THE NEW SCHOOL OF THOUGHT ON IEP & 504 PLANS

Love, Understanding, and Other Best Practices

"Every Child is a Gift"

Larry Martin Davis

ISBN: 145365660X
ISBN 13: 9781453656600

It's time for a new perspective in today's public schools, especially when addressing the needs of exceptional and special needs students. Staff, parents, and students are expected to do so much more but often experience little in return with traditional intervention models. "Love, Understanding, and Other Best Practices" provides a transformative framework for educators on the intervention path, especially those working with parents through IEP and 504 Plans. Special Education directors, staff, teachers, and their General Education colleagues, will discover insight, inspiration, and easy-to- implement strategies in this book. You will learn how to maximize creativity, innovation, and resourcefulness with a relationship-centered approach toward accommodations and specially designed instruction: A change of heart creates a world of difference, one child at a time!

Love, Understanding, and
Other Best Practices

**The New School of Thought
On IEP & 504 Plans**

Larry Martin Davis

"To accomplish great things, we must not only act, but also dream; not only plan, but also believe." —*Anatole France*

TABLE OF CONTENTS:

"Educating the mind without educating the heart is no education at all." Aristotle

PRELUDE

We live in an ever-changing world: Life is moving fast. Don't you feel it? I do. At the same time, our educational system seems to be moving backwards, lagging far behind technology and other social and cultural developments. It's not because we aren't trying and giving it our best. We are. However, our schools are guided by politics and an undermining agenda, with a stagnant set of national academic standards at the core: "The standards were created to ensure that all students graduate from high school with the skills and knowledge necessary to succeed in college, career, and life, regardless of where they live." Fundamentally, the premise behind the Common Core is a predetermined vision of the future, our children, and *their* future. This framework does not resonate with me when I consider the rapid changes within our society. Can we really know what's in our children's best long-term interest when life is changing at the speed of light? I don't believe so.

In contrast to the intent of the Common Core and it's politically inspired vision, no matter how hard we try, teachers everywhere feel as if we're on a never-ending treadmill, falling farther behind and unable to keep up. This is one of the most frustrating perspectives guiding our industry, and it's even more evident within Special

Education. However, I try to keep this in perspective and remember that we *do* make a difference in our students' lives. For the true definition of a "successful life" cannot be measured by standards, assessments, or other quantifiable variables alone. Success, guided by a purpose-driven passion and calling, is led by our hearts, not by our heads. And within the context of "making a difference," the relationships we create represent the measure of our success. Simply stated: good teaching is relationship-guided. So is the intervention process!

Think about it: When you reflect upon the best teachers you ever had, likely those who come to mind are those who created a life-impacting relationship with you and other students. Their gifts to us were less about what was taught and more about the way they compassionately connected us to the gifts and talents within ourselves. So instead of chasing the Holy Grail of education through standards-based assessments alone, I suggest we stop and take care of ourselves and one another through appreciation and gratitude. By highlighting where we are rather than focusing blindly on where we are going, we can best identify what already works now before moving on to the next "best practice." In fact, our educational system is founded upon the premise of diminishing our past efforts while at the same time selling us a new set of "best practices" every year.

Over a thirty-five year career in public education, I have seen more reforms, more "new curricula," and more research-developed initiatives than I've seen in any other industry. And yet all these initiatives have left us with so little in return. The true measure of our success as educators cannot be assessed by the ever-changing guidelines created by politicians and publishers. Our success can only be truly measured by the relationships we develop. The way we feel and the connections we build to one another will stand the test of time. This is especially true within an ever-changing society. Our best efforts support the development of each student's gifts and talents through meaning-centered approaches to learning.

So you may ask, how does this all relate to Special Education, IEP, and 504 Plans? Mr. Einstein said it best years ago: "No problem can be solved from the same level of consciousness that created it. We must learn to see the world anew." The shift of consciousness we need comes from a heart-centered approach, one co-created by a collaborative process of many different people. Specifically, as IEP and 504 teams partner together, an inspired, uplifting conversation can guide the process toward new levels of innovation, creativity, and problem solving. And this book, *Love, Understanding, and Other Best Practices,* will help you get there! For the promise found within each child can only be supported by the infinite possibilities that arise from our collaborative efforts as educators, staff members, and parents. Within the context of intervention, be it in the form of a 504 Plan or specially designed instruction guided by an IEP, our best efforts *do* make a difference in a child's life. It's all about love *and* understanding.

Thank you for joining us on this path.

The road less traveled.

INTRODUCTION: THIS IS A SCHOOL, A CLASSROOM—NOT A FRICKIN' CAR DEALERSHIP!

If you are new to education, welcome aboard, and thank you for taking a brief detour on the road less-traveled by reading this important book. Hopefully, I will change your mind—not about teaching or education, but about how you work with families and their children on the special-needs path. Your initial leap of faith to become a teacher presents an exciting set of opportunities and allows you to truly make a difference in the lives of others. This book will provide the necessary tools required to create relationship as the essential platform supporting your career.

Within the guiding principles found in *Love, Understanding, and Other Best Practices*, you will discover an extraordinary foundation for student learning, but more important, you'll find an inspirational approach to relationships, one that can establish you as a remarkable teacher and also as an extraordinary person! The students you meet on this path promise to be some of the most amazing people you will ever know. For every child is truly a gift, and we have the opportunity to discover something magical within each one. Though common knowledge tells us to be headstrong and guided by our intelligence, it is through our hearts where we make the greatest connection and contribution. In the process, you will also learn more about yourself by teaching special-needs kids. By choosing this book, your instincts have lead you in the right direction. I am honored to share *Love, Understanding, and Other Best Practices* with you.

* * *

Whether you have been teaching for a number of years or you are a veteran staff member, thank goodness this guidebook finally made it to you. You and your colleagues may have been struggling with the direction education is headed: The whole notion of federally mandated curriculum, high-stakes testing, and teacher evaluation systems may be pushing you to think twice about being a teacher or educator. Then, when addressing the ever-increasing special needs population within your district and school, I imagine typical IEP and 504 meetings drive you absolutely crazy. Let's be honest: The traditional meeting format and related intervention process often feels like selling cars. You're trying to convince parents to buy into something you know deep within your heart may not be in their child's best interest.

Do you ever feel you have lost touch with the fundamental reason you got into this profession in the first place? Certainly your dream was not to spend endless hours pushing paper, writing goals and objectives that have no meaning, and fretting about compliance deadlines.

Be honest with yourself: it's time for a change. I don't mean a career change, but rather a shift to an inspired, uplifting perspective and a new way of seeing the big picture. Simply, the old special education paradigm doesn't work any more.

As the saying goes, "What you see is what you find," and coming to work every day with the following limiting perspectives everywhere you look can take a toll:

- "It's about meeting standards; we cannot really focus on each child and their needs."

- "There's never enough money and resources to do the job."

- "Our students come from broken homes; what can we do?"

If anything is broken, it's the system, and I believe it needs its own intervention. That's why this book has been written for you, the teachers and administrators committed to doing the right thing but who are overwhelmed by the education bureaucracy and endless uphill battles. I share your concern about your ability to make a difference within the context of today's politics—so much so that I wrote this book.

Thank you for opening yourself to the possibility of something altogether different: an inspirational perspective with specific strategies called *Love, Understanding, and Other Best Practices.*

- **The initial steps begin by understanding the parent perspective first and foremost.** Genuine collaboration and partnership starts with understanding another's perspective. Within IEP and 504 Plan development, school-to-home partnership is your starting point, and a true heart-driven sense of understanding is your go-to tool within the intervention process. Your success as a teacher and administrator depends on the relationships you establish. Understanding provides the foundation.

- **Second, shifting from ego and self-interest to understanding others is true love personified.** An authentic demonstration of love highlights acceptance and unconditional appreciation of others; anything less is not love or compassion. Love is not about self-interest, ego, and a false sense of control: You may love your job or your students, but true love is demonstrated by understanding another without an expected return on your investment of time or care. Simply, an open heart creates the context of partnership while an open mind supports innovation.

- **During the initial stages of establishing a collaborative process between home and school, mutual understanding remains your primary goal as you guide the team through the evaluation process and fundamental Present Levels of Performance.** By creating common ground through a collaborative set of understandings and insights about the student, the team can navigate the intervention

4

process in one cohesive direction. Without mutual understanding, the foundation of your efforts will fail. Again, it's not about meeting deadlines, writing compliance reports, or establishing annual goals; creating mutual understanding across the table will yield benefits way beyond your expectations.

- **Through an evidence-based approach to decision making, you and your team make steady progress as you wade through collected data together, objectively.** By removing emotion and subjectivity from the process and moving agendas and self-interest off the table, the team can move forward with solid decisions, interventions, and innovative ideas based upon data and quantifiable evidence. An effective IEP and 504 process is best handled when emotions and varying agendas are first identified, addressed, and respected. However, a data-driven process that highlights assessments, tests, charts, and classroom-based evidence will consistently prove to be the best guide for your team.

- **Furthermore, the benefit of a collaborative effort is best discovered within a strength-based process known as appreciative advocacy: a "can-do" approach to IEP and 504 Plan intervention.** By doing so, you are creating bridges toward success, for people achieve so much more individually and collectively from a positive "what works" perspective. In addition, appreciative advocacy highlights that every child is a gift. It inspires extraordinary innovation and creativity within the intervention process due to the overarching principles of promise and potential. As such, appreciative advocacy supports student learning and guides IEP and 504 Plans that work.

- **Finally, authentic collaboration and cooperation develop within the context of transparency; highlighting disclosure of information, resources, and concerns.** Let go of the impulse to manage the decision process and choose to be transparent in order to create an open approach to communication between stakeholders. By striving for real collaboration and cooperation and leaving fear, worry, and control behind, your team will walk the inspired road-less-traveled, not the traditional intervention path. As a result, when an IEP and 504 process is founded upon unconditional love and understanding (and other best practices), the paradigm shifts. The notion of "us versus them" diminishes as the development of "we" is encouraged. True transformation unfolds as the team believes in trust and faith within the whole group as each member lets go of their own agenda of control and worry. Being open with ideas, thoughts, resources, and an honest approach to concerns supports this process.

* * *

Though this book targets educators, it's beneficial for parents as well. Parents are the one constant within an ever-changing process in their child's life, especially those who face the uphill struggle of waking up each day to the challenges of a special needs child. Unless parents chose foster care or adoption, they probably didn't anticipate bringing up a child with autism, ADD, Down Syndrome, or any other neurological disability. Either way, if you're parenting such a child, this is the path you have been given. As a result, you are probably bombarded with a list the length of a football field of things to do for your child. So I would like to share a perspective based upon compassion and experience with you:

Parenting a special needs child is an extraordinary path highlighted by grace, love, and understanding, whether you know it or not. It has been an honor working with these parents as each one faces the challenges of raising an exceptional child. As a result, I have learned three prevailing lessons through this work.

You are up for the challenge, *even though at times it is a struggle and you feel life has not been fair.*

You are blessed with the opportunity to truly transform *not only your child's life but possibly your own. Though at times, you probably wish things were different, and going back to the way things were may seem appealing, especially financially.*

You are not alone, *though at times you may feel like you are the only one going through this experience.*

For those parents who are unfamiliar with special education and the IEP or 504 processes, a complimentary handbook, *The Insider's Guide to Special Education Advocacy,* serves as a wonderful resource for you as you walk this path. However, the following brief definitions may assist parents as you move through the rest of this book.

IEP: *An Individualized Education Plan specifically written for students with an identified disability which impacts learning. Following a formal evaluation process, once the need for Specially Designed Instruction (SDI) through Special Education services is determined, an IEP is developed with parent participation.*

Section 504 Plan: *Similar to an IEP, a 504 Plan is an accommodations plan developed for General Education students who face the challenges of an identified disability that is impacting learning. The significance of the impact requires modifications, adjustments, and accommodations within the regular classroom but does not require specially designed instruction and Special Education services. Like an IEP, the Section 504 Plan is based upon an evaluation process determining eligibility (without SDI).*

* * *

The purpose of *Love, Understanding, and Other Best Practices* is absolutely clear: helping teachers and administrators create a transformative shift in schools within the IEP/Section 504 process. Ideally, this book was written for educators on the inside when working with parents from the outside; by creating a bridge of understanding between the two. As more students are identified with neurological disabilities at epidemic levels and face learning challenges, the intervention process, highlighted by IEP and 504 plans, will be a common experience for more kids and their parents than ever before. This book seeks to help staff and parents successfully walk this path together. Specifically, the handbook guides teachers and staff in their relationships with parents through inspired collaboration to ultimately arriving at a successful intervention. Most notably, *Love, Understanding, and Other Best Practices* establishes enlightening, uplifting perspectives of cooperation, understanding, and transparency that contrast with the old-school paradigm of fear, hidden agendas, and resource scarcity. This book is written to inspire you, encourage you, and help you get back in touch with the fundamental reason you love this job: You love the kids! Therein lies the most powerful tool of all, for true love is understanding.

Warning: This is not a technical book about writing iron-clad goals and objectives or a how-to guide to implement No Child Left Behind, IDEA 2004, Common Core, or any other mandate. It definitely is not a traditional "best practice" guide. In fact, the nature of this book will probable frustrate those who seek quick answers to difficult questions within the IEP or Section 504 process. Also, this book is not specifically about "research-based" strategies to make teachers' jobs easier; it's about creating a collaborative platform between schools, parents, administration, and community.

There's nothing easy about the work General Education and Special Education teachers do. Today's students are not simple to educate; "complex" describes the challenge more accurately. Complex kids require so much more than one-size-fits-all interventions. That's why this book is not about a system of simple interventions, for nothing is trouble-free when addressing the needs of exceptional kids. True intervention requires a collaborative, transparent process between parents and staff. Most importantly, this book is about mutual understanding and establishing a "can-do" attitude that's beyond the scope of a few but within the collective vision of many.

However, I do need to highlight a precautionary insight upfront before you invest time in this book: I understand I may initially step on a few toes and upset the cart in the process. In particular, Special Education directors and staff who are invested in the traditional tried and true system may disagree with my approach. I know many of them personally, and I respect the great challenge put forth within their job descriptions. And I admire the good intentions behind their actions. Nevertheless, many Special Education directors— the folks who are responsible for creating the tone in a school district's special programs—facilitate IEP and Section 504 processes through traditional, old- school paradigms often unstated but clearly evident based upon IEP decisions, program planning, and staffing models:

10

- There are way too many kids being served within IEP or 504 Plans than our system can handle. We are overextended.

- State and federal laws and employee contracts have established mandates and guidelines we must work with, often without appropriate funding, so our resources are limited.

- By opening up the process for one parent by establishing a new precedent, this will likely create a flood of parents making requests the system cannot support.

- Overall, the Special Education department cannot make sweeping changes due to budget limitations and compliance guidelines unless program-related practices, procedures, and policies are supported at the state and federal level. Furthermore, everyone will not be happy, for the system cannot meet the needs of all students through individualized requests by parents. (Sometimes these requests are handled through "hold-backs"; instances when the district holds back services and support unless push comes to shove.)

Consider the following story about Kyle to illustrate this point: I cannot tell you how many times I have seen "hold backs" in Special Education services as if we were negotiating the purchase of a new car. Kyle's story, like all the others shared, are real, however, due to confidentiality, the names have been changed.

I attended a meeting many years ago in what later would be known as the epicenter of Autism Central—walking distance to the Microsoft corporate campus in Washington State. Jill and her husband moved here from California; he was a software engineer from Silicon Valley and she was a stay-at-home mother. Their son had a file as thick as a suitcase, for he had been extensively evaluated since he first demonstrated the early signs of "being different" when he was eighteen months old. At first, Kyle was diagnosed with a developmental delay because he did not talk. Later, as a kindergarten student, he had the classic conditions associated with Asperger's and required an extensive IEP: social/receptive language and social skills highlighting specially designed instruction. All the evaluations from outside service providers stated the same recommendations: "Needs support of an IEP."

As the meeting started, the school-based intervention team clearly identified the meeting as a "student study team" without a specific objective, in contrast to the parents' initial request for a formal evaluation. This meeting did not appear to be a step in parent's intended direction. Within minutes the hidden agenda became apparent; the meeting was facilitated as an accommodations conversation, supported through a 504 Plan. There was no evidence that we would be moving in the direction of an evaluation, though the parents had requested one. Guided by the school psychologist, with no one else talking, the parents' concerns were diminished and dismissed one after another by a number of statements, including "He is just in kindergarten … he needs time like many of the other boys." Finally, after listening for forty-five minutes to the endless stream of dialogue and an oral reading of the 504 Plan document as if it were the owner's manual of a 2003 Honda Accord, I finally stepped in with documentation: evaluations, recommendations, and emails from the teachers who all shared the same point: He needed help. The impairment was *severe enough to warrant an IEP and specially designed instruction." Within minutes, the Special Education director reached into her briefcase and presented the paperwork for a formal IEP Evaluation with the student's name and all related information already written in, even though we'd spent 90% of the meeting addressing a 504 Plan. Just like the scene in "The Wizard of Oz" when the curtain was pulled back, the Special Education director was at first caught off guard but immediately recovered and initiated the evaluation process. And so we immediately moved from a boiler-plate 504 Plan to a formal evaluation following the presentation of evidence, data, and assessments. The decision process quickly shifted from one agenda to another, guided by an <u>evidence-based approach</u> and a fast-paced, developed sense of <u>mutual understanding</u> across the table.*

I see this all the time! It is not unusual for the intervention process to be a roller coaster ride between the minimum services and support initially offered and the "hold back" resources presented later in the meeting. It's a little like buying a new car when the desired vehicle doesn't show up on the lot until the buyer is ready to walk out of the showroom. Unless the parents push the envelope, bring an advocate, or the student is deemed highly inconvenient (more on this later), the traditional, old paradigm tends to work from a "do less" perspective, rather than a "can-do" point of view. Fortunately, Kyle is now on an IEP with appropriate support.

It's fair to state this is a simplistic interpretation of the Special Education director's mindset. However, I have seen this in almost every district across the country: I've been a Special Education advocate for over seventeen years and a principal for another ten; in total, I have been in education for over thirty years. As I see it, the

IEP/504 process often feels confrontational and disingenuous due to an unnecessary tone associated with resource scarcity, a tendency to see kids from a budget-management perspective, and a culture of "hold backs" when working with parents. You, the staff member in the trenches, working the front line with parents and kids, are influenced by a fear-based perspective as well. Rarely do I hear Special Education and General Education teachers say what they really believe or speak as if the child in question was their own kid. Unless you are a veteran teacher working successfully in Special Education for many years, you probably worry about your job status, budget cuts, and compliance reviews. You have been given the impossible task of serving the needs of way too many complex kids with extraordinary needs despite your limited resources. **Remember, fear and worry are often an unwelcome guest at the center of every IEP meeting**. You are not alone. Your students' parents bring their own set of fears and challenges to the meeting; often more than you can ever imagine.

One of the most important shifts toward genuine transformation of the IEP/504 process is your authentic understanding of the parent perspective. Fundamentally, your ability to communicate your insights, celebrations, and concerns depends on the connection between you and your students' parents. Your starting point in every successful IEP and 504 Plan meeting requires you to walk in your parents' shoes before guiding them in a whole new direction.

Notes:

14

PARENTING A SPECIAL NEEDS CHILD: BROKEN KIDS & BROKEN HEARTS?

As an education advocate, I help parents navigate through the Special Education maze. By the time most parents contact me, they are at their wits' end and feel absolutely frustrated by the bureaucracy and insensitivity of the IEP and 504 Plan process. I hear stories of extraordinary pain, sorrow, and frustration daily. But most importantly, I walk away from the conversations understanding that most parents want to be heard, listened to, and understood. Sure, the intensity of a special-needs parent can feel like gale-force winds blowing through a mobile home park, leaving devastation in their path. But at the same time, compassion and understanding on the receiving end can make a significant difference. In terms of fear and worry, as a Special Education staff member you are not alone in this process. In fact, your parents often bring to the meetings a much deeper level of worry, grief, and stress than you can ever imagine unless you walk in the shoes as a special needs parent yourself. I want to share a different perspective with you to help create a better sense of understanding between staff members, administrators, and parents.

I know Marla loved her son very much. She also struggled with being the parent of a special-needs child. Their lives together had never been an easy road. Looking back, she'd never wanted anything as much as the birth of her only child. By the time her son was born, Marla had made sure the household was in perfect order. Her preparations were fueled by her dreams and hopes. She personally painted his room blue during her third trimester, equipped the nursery with every new baby gadget possible, and she and her husband completed Lamaze class like "A" students—they never missed a class and studied as if they were preparing for a final exam. By the ninth month, everything was set and ready to go; there was nothing left to do except to love their son with unlimited devotion.

Marla's son entered the world kicking and screaming and had not given up the fight ever since. Nonstop colic lead to uncontrollable tantrums, which turned to sleepless nights. Sleep deprivation had been a battle ever since the first week. Five years later, Marla and her husband were absolutely exhausted and emotionally spent. Sometimes they even questioned if it was worth "giving up their old life." Their son had an ADHD/ ODD diagnosis at five.

Now with kindergarten on the horizon, Marla was looking forward to a break in her day. In fact, she registered her son for the all-day program, though she was uncertain if he could make it through the first hour alone, for his daycare was running out of options. By the time her son turned five, every preschool in town knew him like they knew a hit-and-run accident. Fortunately, his medications had stabilized things a bit, a doctor's appointment followed school's start, and all she could think was, "I need a break." Every now and then, like a rainbow following a downpour, she saw her beautiful son as he truly is: a gift to the world. Then, like magic, the fleeting thought disappeared. She was emotionally spent and drained from parenting a special-needs child. In her darkest hour, she asked God, "Why me?"

Unless, a parent is blessed with super-human strength and fortitude, most special-needs parents ask the same question: "Why me?" Can you imagine the sense of guilt and shame one experiences in these difficult moments? I can. It humbles me to my knees when I look at my own family and compare the challenges I face parenting typical children with parenting a child with high-needs autism, ADHD, ODD, CP, MS, or any other disability. Besides establishing a learning disability at school, these conditions have a huge impact on the family's day-to-day life and stability. Too many times I have attended IEP or 504 Plan meetings where the result is pre-determined by the staff, and the process looks more like rubber-stamping than a genuine collaborative exchange of ideas and understanding. These cases often lead to a "sign and whine" experience for parents, many of whom often feel rushed not heard. Their concerns and their fears are sometimes diminished and not addressed when deadlines, compliance issues, and an overwhelming paper-trail takes precedence. Like Marla, many parents bring to the IEP or 504 Plan process a deep sense of emotional fragility due to the sense of grief and loss associated with their child's struggles at school.

Often the traditional paradigm supports minimizing the disability and diminishing the impact of a child's struggles. The level of insensitivity I observe astounds me when the process requires parents to prove that their child is failing even though the problems are directly connected with a well-documented diagnosis.

As I write this, I remember an IEP I attended where the child had been diagnosed with Tourette syndrome, OCD, anxiety, and ADHD—the perfect storm, all documented by recent evaluations. During the meeting the parents heard from the school that their daughter was "doing fine," even though in recent reports the teacher notated a need for "constant redirecting," "social concerns," and general distractibility. Who wants to "prove" their daughter has a disability like this? What kind of thinking causes school personnel to be so insensitive that parents often feel like they are going to the judge and asking for forgiveness or understanding? It's time for a change. Within the context of an ever-growing population of special needs kids, the idea that the school serves as judge, jury, and service provider fails to bring about true collaboration and partnership due to misguided underlying principles: fear, hidden agendas, and resource scarcity.

Probably the most enlightening principle guiding our work together within the new IEP/504 paradigm is that true love is understanding, an idea which will be addressed in the next chapter in greater depth. Through an authentic lens of empathy and understanding, our work within the IEP and 504 process takes off in a whole new direction, one where parents and staff establish a genuine path toward collaboration and partnership. I strongly suggest that before you meet with parents, you shift your perspective from a task-oriented, deadlines-driven, and self-centered outlook to a more global understanding of the parent perspective. True partnership comes from the heart.

Specifically, I urge you to set aside your desire to meet compliance guidelines, sign- off, or other intentions that may be about you and your interests as case manager or director. Instead, try to achieve a heartfelt understanding of the parents' perspective. You're familiar with the lighthearted statement, "It's all about me." In these situations, it's all about *them*; our students and their children, who needun your help.

For perspective, consider that in Special Education, one constant holds true from district to district, from school to school: Parents of special-needs children often feel personally responsible for their child's failure within the public school system. In fact, many parents maintain an unyielding focus on "fixing" their child at all costs. They believe there's always a cure just around the corner; it's just a matter of finding it. I see this every day as an education advocate. The contrast between typical parents and special-needs mothers and fathers can be startling. While so-called "typical" families experience public education like a Kodak-moment slideshow, joyfully attending open houses, holiday performances, school carnivals, and science fairs, parents of special-needs children anxiously wait for the phone to ring, their response at the ready: "What has Susan done today?" Living with an endless stream of emails from frustrated teachers and principals, and worse, the humiliating phone calls with requests to "immediately pick up your son," take its toll.

Then there's the nonstop shuttling between physicians, therapists, counselors, and other fix-it activities which not only impact the pocketbook but leave an indelible mark on a parent's perception of their child. Feeling broken is not the place that fosters dreams and inspires greatness. Not only are their children considered broken, but many of these parents have broken hearts as well, as they discover that the initial dreams they had for their children are crushed.

The essence of love and compassion is understanding,
the ability to recognize the physical, material, and psychological suffering of others, to put ourselves "inside the skin" of the other.

We "go inside" their body, feelings, and mental formations,
and witness for ourselves their suffering.
Shallow observation as an outsider is not enough to see their suffering.

We must become one with the subject of our observation.
When we are in contact with another's suffering,
a feeling of compassion is born in us.
Compassion means, literally, "to suffer with." — Thich Nhat Hahn

I've found that many parents of special needs kids experience a common process of loss and grief when their child faces a disability. This is most evident if the consequences of the challenges are significant and the expectations for parenting are on hold or altogether untenable. For example, parents of children on the autism

20

spectrum often experience a huge sense of loss when their child goes inward and doesn't demonstrate cuddling, playfulness, and similar social interaction that many of us long for as parents. Similarly, for parents of intense kids with ADHD, something as simple as going to the bathroom alone or even going shopping becomes impossible if their son or daughter must touch everything in sight or run throughout the house or store at full speed like a hurricane. In these situations, parents often face disappointment when addressing their initial expectations, hopes, and dreams of parenthood. As a result, many move through a loss and grief process as reality sets in. Before a revitalized perspective of acceptance and love develops toward their beloved child, each parent may need to naviagate through their new life's struggles differently and at their own pace. So when you work with your students' parents, you are probably meeting families that are living somewhere on the loss and grief continuum (see the end of chapter for more details).

Years ago, I met a woman, Laura, whose daughter was one of the most amazing kids I have ever met. Jillian was one of those savant types; she knew things that very few of us would either be interested in or capable of knowing. In addition, Jillian exhibited a wide range of delays in all areas of her development, including difficulty with close attachments and an inability to express emotions. This was very challenging for her mother, who was a loving parent. Nevertheless, it was Jillian's extraordinary gift that caused me to think about God's intentions with a five-year-old who clearly had unique interests.

When Laura told her daughter's story, it started out with the usual autism theme; her five-year-old created elaborate schemes involving her dolls and a make-believe play-land where every doll had an important role, special powers, and their own language. Jillian would literally lose herself in this world of fantasy. This is something most parents would be proud of, for it sounded so harmless, though elaborate. As she continued to talk about her daughter, however, tears began to fall down Laura's cheeks. Laura was deeply saddened by the feeling of detachment from her daughter's own little world. Laura also expressed a sense of grief in knowing her daughter would never be "normal." What Laura wanted was so simple: the opportunity to lovingly hold her daughter and experience joy in their relationship. Instead, Laura felt alone. Her daughter often lived in her own world, and instead of being her bundle of love, Jillian was distant and extremely complex. As the story unfolded, it appeared that her five-year-old was remarkably able to identify different flights, scheduled times, and specific airlines servicing our local airport when she was told any location of departure. In addition, Jillian described the specific airplane flown for each departing flight, including the seating arrangement for each plane. I was floored by the focus of her unbelievable talents. Afterwards, I told myself, "God has a very specific plan for this young lady." At that time, however, God's intentions were not clearly known by her mom, who was still experiencing loss and grief. Broken dreams and often broken hearts are common with parents who are parenting at this intense level. This is one of the reasons why parents of special-needs kids may experience extraordinary levels of stress in their personal lives and may even experience divorce at a higher rate than other parents.

A few years later, I ran into Laura and her daughter at a special education fair. After the usual initial greetings, I asked

Laura directly, "What is Jillian's 'thing' these days?" She lit up with a smile as wide as the Grand Canyon as she told me, "We are so into bugs!" She then informed me that her daughter was obsessed with insects and was classifying and categorizing bugs twenty-four hours a day, seven days a week. She spoke to me with immense joy and love and could not hold back her enthusiasm for her daughter's passion. "Jillian loves everything and anything all about bugs … I love that about her!" Our conversation was brief; Jillian wanted her mother's attention since there were many more interesting things to explore than listening to two adults catch up. I was absolutely overjoyed by Laura's update.

What stands out is how much Laura appeared to appreciate and understand her daughter that day, in direct contrast to the first time we met, when Laura was emotionally devastated. Rather than focusing on the absurd nature of her daughter's gift, Laura basks in it. In fact, Laura's love for her daughter truly radiates! But I also know this developed over time, for a broken heart needed to mend.

This story reminds me of my own experience as a parent when I walked the Section 504 (accommodations) path on behalf of my son. Like Laura, I also held a deep level of loss and grief within myself. Back then, I focused more on my shortcomings and missteps as a father than the joy I experienced as a dad. I would soldier on as if nothing was wrong, but in doing so, I was protecting myself from the true pain and sorrow, which eventually revealed themselves. The importance of this insight is something that every educator working both IEP and Section 504 meetings needs to know: What you see as you look at your students' parents probably is not a true reflection of how they feel entering the special-needs arena. I have learned as an education advocate as well as a parent that as we shift from various stages of loss and grief, we may unconsciously try to mask our sorrow. As a result, emotions surface during these intervention sessions, and the process may take on a whole different look.

When my son was in high school, I had tried to wear two hats within the 504 Plan process: both parent and advocate. I was negotiating my son's accommodation plan, something I would not recommend to just anyone. Juggling the information alone can be more than most people can bear. You'd figure that as someone who does this every day for other kids, it would have been a snap for me. This was far from the truth. For one, staff members, particularly the school psychologist, were playing the minimizing game, stating that my son was "doing well considering he had an average IQ." When I asked to see the specific sub-tests from the IQ assessment, the "hold backs" and minimizing started coming one at a time in the following order:

First meeting: "We don't have these scores right now; it's in a file and we are unable to access tests at this time. We need another meeting for this."

Second meeting: In reviewing the IQ subtests, the discrepancy gap between my son's verbal comprehension scores (130) and his processing speed (73) was extreme: a 57-point spread between the two. Nevertheless, the following comments were stated, minimizing my perspective: "Though he does present a discrepancy between his sub-tests, when we look at his overall GPA and

24

classroom performance, he is doing as well as his peers. There is no need for an accommodation plan." Again, *this was not the real story. In specific areas, like science and math, he was well below grade level and failed to meet minimum standards on state assessments.*

Finally, after three meetings, his teachers admitted that there was clear evidence that he was struggling in school. But it wasn't till the last meeting, our fourth, where we were engaged in accommodation development when I absolutely lost it. Out of my mouth flew expletive after expletive: "I cannot believe this f—ing s—, this is so f—ing unbelievable that we are still arguing over the significance of my son's challenges after how many weeks now!" I was angry beyond reproach, for not only was I frustrated by the snail-like process but I was also angry with myself for letting things go on this way for years. I felt like I let my son down, especially considering I do this type of negotiation daily for other kids. I can imagine how it feels for parents walking this path for the very first time!

As I stated earlier, most parents feel personally responsible for their child's disabilities and challenges, though they might not be consciously aware of it. We push these feelings by the wayside and offer a whole different presentation of ourselves—until our emotional buttons are pushed, as described in the story above. No matter how hard we try, the emotional stumbling blocks might not be checked at the door when we enter the IEP or 504 plan arena. We bring everything with us: The good, the bad, and the ugly.

Stages of Grief and Loss: A Lens of Understanding ...

Understanding the stages of grief and the accompanying emotional and physical reactions may help in adjusting to a loss or understanding the emotions others may experience.

Parenting a special-needs child often requires family members to say goodbye to preconceived notions of parenting and begin again with a new perspective. This process of growth may create heartache and feel like grief or loss to some parents. Not all individuals move through these stages one after the other, some people instead experience a range of feelings along this continuum and move back and forth between the stages.

Teaching also presents opportunities where loss and grief are experienced. For example, due to budget considerations, sometimes teachers are required to adjust to unwelcome changes, such as increased class size, moving to a new school, having to shift to a new assignment, or seeing a new student with behavior issues create turmoil and chaos within a relatively calm and structured setting. We all experience loss and grief as life presents one change after another.

Stage 1: Denial

Following the loss of a loved one or grief due to traumatic event, denial serves to protect someone from feeling the immediate impact of the initial event. This may

26

be commonplace for parents who recently discovered a diagnosis like autism, CP, MS, or any other life-changing disability. Some common reactions during the denial stage include:

- Shock or numbness, feelings of emptiness; this may look like indifference or a lack of caring.

- Tendency to isolate; attending meetings may be difficult for these folks.

- Maintaining unrealistic expectations for the future of their child; possibly applying typical goals and outcomes toward their children's school achievement when not appropriate.

Stage 2: Anger

As the level of denial decreases, more emotional reactions to the particular event may emerge. Specifically, feelings of unjustness or unfairness about the event or situation are common. Within the context of special needs, some parents may harbor anger toward life in general and channel this toward others. Some common reactions during the anger stage include:

- Questioning why the diagnosis occurred; still functioning in a state of denial.

- A need to assign blame to rationalize the circumstance.

- Accusations towards family members, friends, or school personnel, all of whom may demonstrate perceived uncaring attitudes; parent may express anger toward others "in their way."

Stage 3: Bargaining

During this stage, issues of guilt associated with the loved one are present, and a special-needs parent may cognitively or emotionally attempt to change the outcomes of past interactions. It is not uncommon to unrealistically associate behavior in the past as contributing to the diagnosis or disability with statements such as, "If only I had ..." Some common reactions during the bargaining stage include:

- Intense preoccupation with the past.

- Expressions of "ought" or "should" related to the circumstance.

- Making promises with the intention of bringing about unrealistic events; this often sounds like "We will do ____ every night," but this may not be possible over the long haul.

- Doing everything in one's power to fix the child, no matter what the cost or amount of time; often expecting the school to perform a miracle and do the impossible with limited resources.

Stage 4: Depression

As parents realize that their efforts at bargaining will remain unrealized, an understandable feeling of sadness or loss may occur. Parenting highly complex special-needs kids takes its toll. Some common reactions during the depression stage include:

- Overwhelming feelings of sadness.

- Inability to concentrate and focus; following-through on commitments may be improbable.

- Difficulty making decisions.

- Unexplained mood fluctuations.

Stage 5: Acceptance

Acceptance is considered the final stage in the grief process: understanding the "present levels" of one's children and realizing this does not change one's love for them. A newfound level of appreciation and understanding seems to replace the sense of loss and grief. Some common reactions during the acceptance stage include:

- Talking about the diagnosis/disability positively and realistically; "a gift within."

- Reinvesting emotional energy in other directions instead of "trying to fix things" at all costs.

- Resuming normal activities.

Notes:

THE BATTLE BETWEEN FEAR, SELF-INTEREST, AND TRUE LOVE

Years ago, I discovered an extraordinary book, *True Love: A Practice for Awakening the Heart* by well-known author Thich Nhat Hanh. The Zen Buddhist scholar describes four teachings that guide his readers toward a transformative practice of love and understanding. Essentially, Hanh asks us to be present and to understand our loved ones from the head and heart. Within Special Education, truly knowing the child first and foremost provides the foundation for everything. Evaluations, IEPs, 504 Plans, accommodations, goals/objectives—each step is based upon an extensive understanding of the child. A well-designed IEP or 504 Plan is created upon common ground established within a clearly developed evaluation and "present levels of performance." Most importantly, the practice of true understanding lies in the insights addressing each child's gifts rather than his or her shortcomings and failures alone. Creating a well-written Evaluation or Present Levels of Performance requires one to be present with others, most notably with your students.

I understand this sounds basic, but consider how difficult it is for us to move beyond our own experiences, self-interest, and personal egos when we create a perception or understanding of others. How often do I hear, "We understand autism; we had a student here last year in our class who was just like ..." or "Kids with ADHD always seek out attention ..." or "She reminds me of her brother—the Wilsons are all alike." The intent of comments like these is to demonstrate understanding, but true understanding is a whole different frame of reference. It's about learning how to put aside our personal issues and our own agendas and experiences, and instead seek understanding of each individual student as the primary function of our efforts.

"What must a person do in order to understand a person? We must have time; we must practice looking deeply into this person. We must be there, attentive; we must observe, we must look deeply. And the fruit of this looking deeply is called understanding. Love is a true thing if it is made up of a substance called understanding." Thich Nhat Hanh

As a result, within the IEP or 504 processes, at the core of understanding is this thing called "love." True love *is* understanding. One belief that tends to get in the way of a collaborative process is that educators work from the position of "Doing what's in the best interests of kids," as if teachers have cornered the market on children and their best interests. I read this in every district in every mission statement and every website all across the country. As a former administrator myself, I either wrote this weekly on our school bulletin or heard one of my staff members regularly share this comment across the table during parent meetings. But this is not always true. Most people work from the position of doing what's in their own best interest. This is unconscious human nature at work, and anything different requires the mindfulness of a monk, or at least the guidance of one. Or a therapist.

Don't get me wrong; educators and teachers are generally caring individuals. But human nature is an evolving process where we move from an ego-driven/self-centered perspective associated with childhood wants and needs to a love-based, understanding approach associated with adulthood. The process in between is called "maturity." Educators are on the same path toward maturation as everyone else, though good intentions may be more prevalent amongst educators due to a personal calling many in this profession choose to follow. Nevertheless, we are no different as people, for our actions are based upon our experiences, our needs, and our ego. The pursuit of true love—which ultimately is understanding—is an ongoing process and takes place in the classroom as well as in life itself.

Though the intent of the IEP and 504 process should be about meeting the needs of very complex kids, way too often I hear lots of self-interest expressed outside the scope of understanding of a child's needs. I've often seen...

- *Special Education directors worried about their budgets and the bottom line.*

- *Resource Room teachers diminishing the impact or severity of a child's disability when there are not enough resources readily available.*

- *General Education teachers making the case for immediate placement in Special Education when a student's behavior is disrupting teaching and learning.*

- *Parents afraid to push for services because they fear retaliation.*

- *Parents also making the case for unrealistic services, like instructional aides or private school for their kids, because they read about special services on the Internet, or a friend of a friend's child received special treatment.*

This all needs to stop. In fact, I look forward to the day when the primary purpose of a meeting is no longer to appease everyone's fears, worries, or misguided interests. Instead, we all need to work from a common-ground perspective called "mutual understanding," where possibilities are endless and resources are accessible through co-creation and collaborative problem solving when "evidence-based decision making" takes place and guides the team process from emotion and subjective reasoning to objectivity.

Somewhere between the memories of childhood and the grand illusions we bring to parenthood and teaching, we create perceptions from which we work, both as parents and educators. For example, in looking back, I think I liked the taste of cotton candy, or somehow

I remember it that way. But I tried it a few years ago at the county fair, and I found it too sweet and sticky. Same thing goes for carnival rides. I don't care for them anymore. What was once a thrill is now a total waste of time. My perception (memory, really) was far from the reality. Same goes for many experiences from my early youth. I believe this is the same thing that happens to most parents and teachers when they reflect upon their public school experiences of years ago. Consider the following:

- "The Apple Doesn't Fall Far From the Tree": Many parents with special-needs kids, in looking back over their *own* experiences at school, realize that they struggled in school themselves. This often creates negative emotional memories, and for these folks, the whole experience of going back to school on their child's behalf recreates a wide range of unpleasant emotions.

- "Love What You Know and Know What You Love": For many teachers and staff members, school was a pleasant experience. In fact, school may have established a foundation of positive self-esteem. As a result, some educators cannot relate to the struggles their students experience for learning because their own whole school experience was so rewarding. Some parents, especially those who are new to the elementary school system, often get all warm and fuzzy inside when they smell paste, see a box of crayons, or look at chairs fit for dwarfs. "Circle time," listening to Curious George being read aloud, making

35

Valentines for your friends, and running free at recess for hours on end swirl through these parents' memories.

But then, there is reality. That's where I come in.

As an education advocate, I am often setting parents straight. Somewhere in the conversation, I may need to state:

"Yes, the people who work at schools are nice, often with good intentions, but like everyone, educators sometimes fail to step up to the plate and do what they say. Some are working from self-interest while others may be limited by fear-based beliefs like "Our hands are tied," "If we do this for one child, we will have to do this for everyone," or "There's just not enough money (or time) to do everything under the sun."

Parents who learn the reality lesson the hard way are often those with special-needs kids. Helping parents move from fantasy to reality is a part of my job. In fact, it's also part of *your* job as educators. For it's critical that we help parents understand the real limitations we are all working with. Absolutely, class size, shrinking budgets, and state and federal guidelines are all real issues. In this day and age of Internet access, social media networks, and parent-empowerment, it's best to be straight with parents as well as with ourselves. People can quickly see through false explanations and faulty interpretations. So it's best to keep things simple and allow the evidence to speak its truth. When addressing the needs of each specific child in practice as well as within the

IDEA laws governing special education, our focus needs to be on the child and their needs.

However, when school administrators, special education directors, and teachers project their own issues and self-interests upon the intervention process, an adversarial dynamic is often the result. Sometimes these interactions resemble a scene from the "Little Red Riding Hood" playbook: Imagine an administrator who appears to be a s nice as one's favorite Granny. However, underneath the veiled smile and friendly greeting, there may be a completely different animal: wolf-like, controlling, short-sighted, and at times, ego-driven and self-centered. I would like to tell the tale of "Little Red riding Hood and the Big Bad Wolf," a version from my travels on the road as an advocate. The names have been changed to protect the innocent, but the characters remain true to the story.

Katie, a soft-spoken but strong-as-nails mother of three, asked me to help her as she was negotiating for a 504 Plan (a disability accommodation plan within regular General Education); her middle school son experienced life with ADHD. From the outset, I figured her out fairly quickly; she was a person with strong convictions who believed that people are naturally good. The former attribute functions as a strength as she negotiates for her child's accommodations with grace and kindness, but sometimes her Pollyanna perspective frustrates her. She's gifted with a relentless focus and is unwilling to give up. Throughout the intervention process, she was amazed by the inability of the school administrators to work with her and do what she believed was right for her son. By the time we met, she had already initiated a formal evaluation process in seeking out resources for her struggling child; he was earning D's and F' s in a number of classes as a result of "missing or late assignments." Nevertheless, the school had determined that his disability was not "significant" enough to warrant specially designed instruction through an IEP (Special Education) and was unwilling to support him through a set of accommodations found within a 504 Plan (General Education). As a result, Katie sought my guidance to renegotiate for a 504 Plan.

As I entered the fray midstream, I reviewed the records and documents related to the initial evaluation for the IEP. I discovered the school psychologist failed to follow district and state protocol by not utilizing a cognitive (IQ) assessment, though permission was signed by the parents. The cognitive test provides critical information related to processing skills, often an issue for students with ADHD. The standard assessment, the Weschler Intelligence Cognitive test [WISC], takes up to four hours to administer. So from my perspective, someone was taking shortcuts and not taking the initial evaluation process seriously. It appeared that the school psychologist assumed that Katie's son did not qualify for specially designed instruction prior to the evaluation and felt that he was not really disabled at all; instead he needed a firm kick in the pants to set him straight. I brought this up to the district Special Education director, and she brushed it off as unimportant. With a smile on her face, she stated, "No one would have done this intentionally" and "I understand how frustrated you must feel," always with a smile. The level of condescension was so thick you could cut it with a knife. Throughout the meetings, the Special Education director and her colleague, the assistant principal, always wore a smile just like the Big Bad Wolf did, as if the smile was a mask for some other hidden agenda. Also, they were the only staff members who spoke during our initial meetings.

Weeks passed and endless emails went back and forth. Katie's son continued to fail in class without the support of a 504 accommodation plan. Everyone acknowledged his disability, but the teachers consistently commented at the these meetings that they weren't sure what made Katie's son tick and they did not know how they could really help him. A general lack of understanding prevailed. Of course, if they had appropriately completed the initial evaluation the previous year, information from the cognitive assessment could have helped us address his processing skills and gaps related to learning. I strongly suggested the school reevaluate Katie's son. This idea was immediately shut down by the director, who stated, "This is not possible, for this would legally have to be part of an IEP evaluation process, not a 504 Plan." This was followed by an invitation to start a separate IEP request process afterwards. The hidden agenda was obvious in this situation; the director was doing everything possible to avoid moving forward with a formal evaluation. In the meantime, Katie's son continued to experience missing assignments, penalties for late work, and detention sessions.

One of the most telling moments throughout the process came as the director stated, "I am functioning as a facilitator of the 504 process with no hidden agenda or bias. I am neutral." Fortunately, she was "just a facilitator," when the wisdom of one of the veteran teachers took center stage against the hidden agenda. The veteran teacher took initiative and spoke out. "Katie's son was a classic ADHD student and required a number of accommodations to succeed." The teacher then outlined the accommodation she was currently employing in her class. Fortunately, the rest of the staff followed along and agreed with their colleague once it was established that speaking honestly was safe. Consistently, when truth and understanding rise to the surface, ego and self-centered agendas fall by the wayside. Katie's son received a 504 Plan and was successfully supported by his teachers through appropriate accommodations.

Unfortunately, this frustrating scenario happens more often than you might think. For years, I have received phone calls and emails from parents who describe the same situation, where hidden agendas and self-interest seem to get in the way of a process that needs to be collaborative. I also have to tell parents that they cannot believe what they read on the Internet as absolute truth and what may be an appropriate accommodation or specially designed instruction for one child may not be the best option for their child. The notion of agendas and self-interest goes both ways.

As a result, I recommend that my Special Education colleagues create a *genuine* sense of mutual understanding through the Evaluation and Present Levels of Performance process. By highlighting a well-rounded set of data and evidence as the foundation, and taking time to assure that parents and staff are moving toward mutual understanding, this becomes an important investment of time and resources. Also, genuinely acknowledging parent concerns, worries, and fears prior to the decision process allows the dialogue to move forward toward mutual understanding.

Pre-Meeting Conference

As I stated earlier, parents appreciate the opportunity to let off steam and just be heard. One specific technique which makes a huge difference is to establish a **pre-meeting conversation** between the teacher, case manager, and/or anyone with an established relationship of trust with the parent. This brief conversation, whether in person or on the phone, held prior to the scheduled formal meeting, will serve both sides well.

- Provides parents an opportunity to ask questions without taking valuable meeting time or feeling embarrassed.

- Provides parents and staff an opportunity to review the key notes within the draft documents; best if handled at least 48 hours prior to the meeting.

- Provides parents an opportunity to share their concerns, worries, or fears (which may lead to hidden agendas) within a safer, more comfortable setting.

- Provides staff members opportunity to flush out hidden agendas or other issues which may blindside the team during a meeting; one can prepare accordingly.

Notes:

<u>IEP/504 Planning Checklist</u>: Pre-Meeting Conference Guide

☐ General Education/classroom accommodations: *previously established; IEP or 504*

☐ Disability/diagnosis: *See evaluations from clinicians*

- Specific learning disability:
  _____ (example: reading)

- Health impairment/other:
  _____(example: ADHD)

- Copy of the diagnostic DSM (including typical symptoms)

☐ Data (include copies of the following):

- IQ and achievement evaluations (formal evaluations with scores)

WISC (IQ):   Verbal _____   Perceptual _____

                    Working Memory _____   Processing Speed _____

WIAT/WJR: Oral Expression _____   Listening _____

                    Written Expression _____   Basic Reading _____

                    Reading   Math Calculation
                    Comprehension _____   Skills _____

                    Math Reasoning _____

42

- Medical diagnostic work: neurological report, speech, clinical psychologist

- Academic assessment results: ITBS, Reading Inventory, Dibbles

- Report cards: grades and teacher comments stating areas of concern

- Emails: teacher's areas of concern or previous accommodations

- Discipline records: suspensions, referrals, time-outs

- Proposed or past IEP, 504 plan, or evaluation results: *ask for documents a couple days before the meeting; this allows you to preview what's to come.*

☐ List of previous accommodations and support services

Within the Classroom:

Activity:	Purpose:	Dates: Impact: *example*
After school reading	Increase 9/05-reading fluency	Still below grade

43

_____

_____

_____

_____

_____

_____

Within a "pullout" program or outside of class:

Activity:	Purpose:	Dates: Impact: *example*
After school reading	Increase 9/05- reading fluency	Still below grade

_____

_____

_____

_____

_____

After or before school:

_____

_____

_____

Parent supported services (academic):

_____

_____

_____

Other services or support:

_____

_____

For students with a current or previous IEP:

☐ List the specific areas with Specially Designed Instruction:

Reading__ Math __ Written Language ___ Communication ___ Social Skills___ Behavior___ OT/PT__

Annual Goals: Measured by: Expected Outcome Current Data / Present Levels:

_____ _____ _____ _____ _____

_____ _____ _____ _____ _____

_____ _____ _____ _____ _____

_____ _____ _____ _____ _____

_____ _____ _____ _____ _____

©Larry Martin Davis www.specialeducationadvocacy.org

MUTUAL UNDERSTANDING: HOW TO AVOID DUE PROCESS!

Often, I am asked by parents if they should pursue a 504 Plan or an IEP. I usually say the same thing, "It depends." The decision is based upon the discovery within the Evaluation and Present Levels of Performance discussion. Both IEP and 504 meetings are guided by the same leading questions; we often don't have a preconceived notion of either one of the two interventions unless the student already has an IEP. Fundamentally, IEP and the 504 Plan processes are guided by two different programs; the 504 Plan intervention falls within the General Education umbrella, whereas the IEP process is within the context of Special Education guided by IDEA. I don't worry about the decision for accommodations or specially designed instruction until we complete an evaluation addressing the questions below. Ideally, creating mutual understanding within the evaluation process is our goal and will assist the team in addressing these three critical questions:

1. **Is there an established disability or diagnosis? Or a suspected diagnosis or disability?**

2. **What impact does this disability or diagnosis have on the student's school experience, including academic, social, emotional, or behavior considerations?**

3. **Finally, when considering interventions, how would Specially Designed Instruction through an IEP or accommodations via a Section 504 Plan be most appropriate?**

From my experience, the overarching principle of mutual understanding—establishing genuine knowledge of the child from the parent, educator, and outside service provider perspective—remains the primary focus at the initial discovery stage of the game. Mutual understanding supports a relationship founded upon active listening, consideration, and coherence among stakeholders; whatever affects one participant correspondingly affects the others. As a result, an investment of time within the Evaluation and Present Levels of Performance creates a sense of synergy amongst team members. This often proves to be most valuable as the team moves into the intervention process to follow.

Conflicting perspectives can often create adversarial relationships between home and school. Most frequently, separation and division develops when people come to the intervention table with an established set of beliefs, inflexible mindsets, set-in-stone interventions, and most importantly, pre-determined decisions related to the three questions above. This tends to break down the collaborative process. Some examples adversarial stances are below.

- Adversarial Parent: I cannot tell you how many times parents seek my assistance in "getting an instructional aide" for the child. I soon discover that the parent may have spoken to a neighbor or read something on the Internet about how an aide was the true path to instructional salvation. Sometimes this comes in the form of a parent seeking private school placement. After I bring them back down to earth, I have to explain to them the process is all about creating mutual understanding from the Evaluation to the Present Levels. If there is a glitch along this course of action, you end up with a struggle between parents and staff, though it doesn't need to be this way. Be assured you'll create an adversarial relationship when you make demands from the get-go, at the start of the process.

- Adversarial District: Even more commonly, I attend meetings in which the facilitator glosses over the Evaluation or Present Levels of Performance by reading the document until the time is almost up. This minimizes conversations and the potential for collaborative dialogue. Furthermore, many 504 and IEP meetings are set up as signing events rather than an opportunity to create an authentic sense of partnership between parents and staff. In these situations, members of the staff previously conducted a meeting and decisions were already made. When the insiders are the "experts" or decision-makers— and the parents are expected to capitulate and sign off on the plan without really understanding the nature of the process or their child at school—a non-collaborative model of intervention is created. This a process fails to work within the context of twenty-first century parents, who are often well-informed and empowered.

One of the biggest changes in Special Education over the last twenty-plus years is the shift of parents moving from *spectators* of the decision making process to empowered *advocates and co-collaborators* due to the wealth of information now easily accessed through social networks, the Internet, and support groups. Years ago, special-needs issues were swept under the carpet by most families and addressed quietly, and in isolation amongst themselves. Now, as we continue to evolve within the twenty-first century, sometimes referred as the age of entitlement, Special Education feels like an extension of the civil rights movement. It is not uncommon for parents to share their kid's diagnosis openly and freely. Sometimes I imagine Soccer Moms driving vans with bumper stickers stating, "My Child Has Autism and Yours Doesn't," or "My Kid Is an ADHD Student at Einstein Middle School."

Due to this significant shift in society and culture, parents are now informed consumers and partners. In fact, many are aware of Special Education law and guidelines calling for parent partnership in decision making. **Working from a position that creates mutual understanding keeps districts out of contentious due process hearings and inspires innovation within the intervention process**. We can achieve so much more from a cooperative perspective of many, rather than the limited scope of a few.

50

I believe some educators lose touch with the notion that school can be very trying for many students. Not everyone succeeds within the system, even though many educators, especially teachers and administrators, thrived in the past within the box called "school." For special-needs students and their parents, school presents a challenge: if you don't fit in the standards-driven *round hole*, especially if you are a *square peg*, it is not always an easy path being different. In these cases, a collaborative process, founded upon mutual understanding across the table, is most valued: a gathering of loving, caring, understanding individuals working on the same page for the same cause. Sometimes it takes the leadership of one significant individual to help the group create this shift. One specific case from years ago, one which I will never forget, highlights this case in point: An enlightened principal was that key individual creating a new paradigm for the team to follow:

When I caught up with Lauren and her folks at the annual Special Education IEP meeting, I was immediately taken back by Lauren's grace and style. It had been a year since I last saw her. Her angelic face personified goodness, hope, and determination. Her smile showcased a unique blend of adolescent shyness and an emerging self-confidence. Being sixteen and a junior in high school, Lauren presents herself through a complex intersection of youth and a developing sense of maturity. She is one of a kind; a diamond in the rough.

When we first met years ago, Lauren was a troubled seventh grade student failing classes right and left; according to her teachers, she was disorganized, lacked effort, and failed to "work up to her potential." Though she felt like she gave school her best effort, no matter how hard she tried, she was always behind, she missed assignments, and often felt she didn't understand subjects like math and science. By the time she came home every day, she was exhausted. Her parents barely kept their daughter afloat by assuring she finished the endless backlog of assignments piling up each semester. Sometimes these homework sessions would last for hours and end in a battle of wits between mother and daughter.

Fortunately, Lauren's folks pursued every life support possible for their daughter; she was drowning in failed classes, excessive homework, and a growing sense of dread toward school. At first, after-school sessions at a nationally recognized tutor center was thought to be "the fix." But this was addressing only the symptoms of a more complex issue. From Lauren's perspective, not only was she burned out from school, but adding hours at the tutor each week on top of endless hours of homework actually fried her emotionally by the end of each day. Failing grades eventually took a backseat to a greater concern related to depression. Lauren was feeling overwhelmed.

Her mom commented at the meeting, "I remember this like it was yesterday: you were telling us to yank her out of tutoring because it obviously wasn't addressing her particular problem. After doing so, Lauren looked at me and we both smiled at each other. I never told her, but I hated taking her to tutoring, too. I was just desperate to find something that would help her."

Finally, her parents sought the help of a clinical psychologist. He administered a variety of assessments addressing learning processing, distractibility, and forgetfulness, and he explored their daughter's emotional well-being as well. I first met Lauren and her parents immediately after the ADD Type II Inattentive Diagnosis was discovered and assisted the family by negotiating academic support at school through accommodations and specially designed instruction through an IEP. By seventh grade, Lauren and her family were worn out after years of playing catch-up with never-ending late assignments, overdue projects, and missing homework. Something had to give, for Lauren was turning into an emotional wreck from the pressure of failing classes and poor report cards.

Lauren had always been an artist at heart. Her binder at school was a collection of doodles, detailed drawings, and fashion designs. From a teacher's perspective, she was often described as "impulsive," a "daydreamer," and lacking in self-discipline. They never saw how hard she worked overtime toward improving her grades. Her mother recalled, "In fact, she was accused of being a slacker by some of her teachers (just not to her face). It was told to me by administrators."

After the formal evaluation, which included both academic and processing assessments, we discovered a significant piece of the learning puzzle. Lauren experienced a major challenge with "processing speed"; her tests indicated she was performing at the bottom 5% level compared to her peers on a percentile scale. Processing speed is often one area of a four-part IQ (cognitive) assessment. Specifically, processing speed identifies the amount of time students take to process information through various means, including auditory and visual learning. In Lauren's case, she had experienced difficulty making connections with new learning, directions, and concepts on the first go-round; she often required multiple attempts at grasping the ideas before they were well understood and embedded in her memory. As a result, missing assignments, forgotten directions, unclear expectations, and general forgetfulness had been thought of as the by-product of laziness and not trying hard enough. Her report cards through elementary school and junior high stated these comments.

I remember the evaluation meeting as if it were yesterday. As we started to review the documents together, the facilitator began to read each page word by word. It was clear that we were going to sit through another meeting with little or no discussion. Lauren's parents looked at me in disgust. Then the principal walked in late. I thought this was a bad sign. Immediately after quickly going through the evidence, he stated, "Wow, Lauren reminds me of my son. He had scores [processing speed] just like this." To my surprise, he continued. "Why are we even bothering with a 504 Plan meeting? Let's cut to the chase. This girl needs an IEP."

The meeting went in a whole new direction due to the insights offered by the principal. In fact, I can still see the looks on Lauren's parents' faces: dumbfounded. For the first time in years, someone understood their daughter! Fortunately, a team of teachers followed suit, and everyone within the IEP was on board with a similar understanding of Lauren once the ice was bro ken.

An extensive set of accommodations had been adopted to support Lauren's academic plan focusing on both distractibility (ADD) and processing speed: provide a class set of notes, extend due dates when needed, sign daily assignment planners, and break large projects into meaningful chunks. In addition,

54

her IEP also provided additional support through specially designed instruction in study skills and organization.

Lauren's mother also made it clear that once the IEP was written, Lauren's issues never went away, though it was much easier to help her when the issues were mutually understood beyond "being lazy" and "spacey." So Lauren's mom pursued additional after-school support once again. "We were fortunate to find a great tutor. She had been a godsend! It definitely was expensive as we had her come over three times a week when Lauren needed it, but it was truly an investment in Lauren's future. It also served the very important purpose of allowing me to step out of the primary 'homework Gestapo' role, which was a great relief and helped our relationship."

One of the noticeable things about Lauren was her innate personal sense of fashion. She had style! In my years of knowing her, she consistently presented herself with a new hairstyle, unusually creative outfits, and a flair for the unconventional. When she smiled, she radiated. Also, she was someone who was to be taken seriously, for she has acquired the necessary skills to be an exceptional self-advocate within her education. Due to her understanding of processing speed and distractibility associated with ADD and their impact on learning, she was able to articulate examples of successful instruction within her classes as well as being self-aware of the accommodations that were lacking when learning became most difficult. It was impressive to be in a room of teachers and watch Lauren address her strengths and shortcomings with confidence. Within these meetings, she spoke to the adults with respect, honesty, and an astounding sense of grace. She was truly a blessing to be around.

Years later, as we concluded the last annual meeting I would attend, I saw in Lauren's face a look of patience and understanding years beyond her age, as if she knew the staff were obligated to share their vision of academic success, which included college even though it was not what she had in mind for herself. For she knew within her heart that art called, fashion reached out to her, and creativity was a life force she could not say no to. She made up her mind that she was going to cosmetology school as soon as she could. She saw a career in hair design and makeup in the very near future.

Her mom said it best, "She really is something, isn't she? It is just a matter of time; she will blow them all out of the water with what she is able to accomplish."

As a follow up and in her own words, Lauren writes:

"I really hope that my story can give parents and children inspiration and a little light at the end of the dark tunnel called the public education system. I remember being in their shoes and dwelling on the fact that I was different and I would never be able to achieve my goals in the same manner as everyone else. I recall feeling cursed with this 'disability' [ADD]. No longer does it feel like a curse, for it's the most beautiful gift I have ever been graced with. You helped me to see that."

"I am now employed full time at a Salon in Ballard and living in a house in Seattle with some good friends and my dear fat kitty cat. In addition to the hairstyling, I also make jewelry, accessories, and occasionally hats and I've started selling my creations at swap meets and the salon I work at. About a year ago I had opened up my own small business in Georgetown, which

opened a new door to my latest passion: reflexology massage and crystal energy healing. It has led my life down a wonderful path of positive thinking and the desire to heal the mind and body. What a great feeling to be content with where you are and where you're going in this life."

In looking back, what was most impressive was not what happened, but instead what *could* have happened if the shift toward mutual understanding hadn't taken place.

- Due Process: Before the meeting at the junior high school, Lauren's parents decided that they would pursue legal guidance if there wasn't a shift in support for their daughter. Another year of watching their daughter go deeper into depression due to the school experience was unacceptable to them. Fortunately, due process was never an option needed.

- Depression: In her own words, Lauren stated what so many students have experienced: "I was different and I would never be able to achieve my goals in the same manner as everyone else. I recall feeling cursed with this disability." Depression is a serious consideration when there appears to a major disconnect for our kids. According to a recent article in *Psychology Today* magazine, high school and college students are five to eight times as likely to suffer from depressive symptoms as teenagers were fifty or sixty years ago.

As we walk this path together—as educators, parents, clinicians, and social workers—the intervention process, whether it be a 504 Plan or an IEP, requires collaboration to truly support the numbers of kids today who are facing learning disabilities and social and emotional challenges. The responsibility of facilitating this process is within the policies and practices of the districts and schools themselves. Certainly, it is unreasonable to expect the education community to perform miracles alone. However, in supporting mutual understanding amongst all stakeholders in this process, we do make a difference in the lives of our children. And it's through a simple decision each district, school, and every teacher makes: do we do this alone and potentially create an adversarial relationship with our parents, or do we do this in partnership? Within the procedural safeguards distributed to every parent on this path, due process remains an option—one usually not in the best interest of anyone.

Tools for Consideration: Creating Mutual Understanding Before & During the Mtg.

Before the Meeting:

- Establish a "pre-meeting" with parents to include:

  o Review the IEP/504 Checklist

  o Share "draft" documents

  o Listen a majority of the time

  o Address concerns and issues; establish a time-frame for each that can be addressed

  o Co-create the agenda for the upcoming meeting together

  o Establish meeting times that work out for all members of the team

During Meeting:

- Clarify the purpose of the meeting including projected outcomes and time restraints

- Introduce everyone; include a brief statement of how each member of the team supports the student

- Establish a shared heart-centered moment of appreciation: authentic and inspired, shared by all

- Present Prior Written Notice at end of meeting or establish a delivery time

- Use a visual chart in support of the decision-making process to include:

Sample Meeting Worksheet: IEP or 504 Plan

Attending:

_____ _____ _____ _____ _____

_____ _____ _____ _____ _____

Purpose of meeting: Initial IEP/504   Annual IEP/504 IEP/504 Addendum   Evaluation DISABILITY(S) of concern:

_____

_____

_____

_____

Summary (write a brief statement highlighting child's current levels of performance related to medical diagnosis, school performance, and evaluations):

- Academic/General Education performance (reading/writing/math/other):

  o What works? (*Literally, spending quality time on this conversation*)

60

_____

_____

_____

_____

o   What are her/his challenges?

_____

_____

_____

_____

- Social/Emotional (peer and adult relationships, expressive and receptive language, sense of self-worth, emotional state of mind at school)

    o   What works? (Literally, spending quality time on this conversation)

_____

_____

_____

_____

    o   What are his/her challenges?

_____

_____

_____

_____

- Cognitive (intelligence): Formal assessments as measured by WISC or other evaluation tools

WISC (Ability)	Score	Comments:
Verbal Comprehension	_____	_____
Perceptual Reasoning	_____	_____
Processing Speed	_____	_____
Working Memory	_____	_____

o Strengths within the cognitive assessments:

_____

_____

_____

o Challenges as evaluated:

_____

_____

_____

WIAT/WJR (Achievement):   Score Comments:

Reading	__ __ __ __	_____
Math	__ __ __ __	_____
Written Language	__ __	_____
Listening	__ __	_____
Oral Language	__ __	_____

o Strengths within the assessments:

_____

_____

_____

_____

62

o Challenges within the assessments:

_____

_____

_____

_____

_____

• Physical: Health, wellness, activities

_____

_____

_____

_____

• Interests (outside of school): "Bridging" activities to his/her success at school

_____

_____

_____

_____

_____

• Accommodations within the General Education setting currently in place:

Accommodation:	Facilitator:	Purpose:
Seating, adjusted assignments	*Teachers*	*Increase focus*

_____

_____

_____

_____
_____
_____
_____
_____
_____
_____
_____
_____
_____
_____
_____
_____

- Specially Designed Instruction (IEP) currently in place:

SDI:	Facilitated By:	Purpose/Goal:	Measured by:
Study skills class, teachers	*Increase reading*	*4th grade level*	*Brigance Test*

_____
_____
_____
_____
_____
_____
_____
_____
_____
_____
_____

- Accommodations within General Education setting PROPOSED:

Accommodation: Facilitator: Purpose:

Seating, adjusted assignments   *Teachers*   *Increase focus*

- Specially Designed Instruction (IEP) PROPOSED:

SDI: Facilitated By: Purpose/Goal: Measured by:

Study skills class, *Increase reading* *4th grade level*   *Brigance Test*

teachers

- Next Meeting:

Date:	Purpose of Meeting	Information/Resources Needed for Meeting:
Oct. 28	Review behavior plans	Suspensions, class discipline, referrals

NOTES:

EVIDENCE BASED DECISION: LET THE TRUTH BE TOLD!

It is often so difficult to figure out what is "the truth" or "best interests" when discussing learning disabilities. There are so many complex variables as well as intense emotions in the mix. Everyone makes a good case in support of their personal perspective, and often we hear "research based" as the rationale for everything proposed by district staffers. (As a side note, I can show you research making the case in support of chewing gum as a "best practice.") Nevertheless, if there is a genuine sense of mutual understanding created amongst stakeholders, staff, parents, and students, then all parties work collaboratively from a fundamentally agreed-upon perspective rather than from each member's own definition of best interests. That's where evidence-based decision making comes in.

For example, when considering the impact of ADD for one of my client's kids, an adopted teenager who failed to complete assignments regularly, many conflicting perceptions were brought to the table. Each person made a strong case from their perspective:
Parents: "*Our son is burned out by the time he gets home after school. Self-regulating [impulsivity] all day during school is exhausting. He is ready to just let go and be a kid. We don't*

see the point of doing homework and fighting that battle every night, for he primarily unloads his emotional backfill at home; we are not his teachers, we are his emotional support."

Counselor: *"It is common for teenagers to rebel against their parents; I imagine it's almost impossible to get him to do anything. He is a classic boy; my son is the same."*

General Education teacher: *"In class he participates in discussion and seems to enjoy the activities. In class, he earns consistent B grades but fails to do any work outside of class as well as projects. I struggle with letting go of the basic requirements expected of all students, so I cannot let him slide. It's just that the completion of assignments are essential to learning."*

Resource Room Teacher: *"We have created a file system for his work, and we check his planner every day. How he fails to turn in the assignments is a mystery to me; he needs someone at home making sure the assignments are getting done."*

Everyone made sense. Most usually do. Also, lots of good intentions were expressed. At least, each part of the puzzle seems to hold a bit of truth. Then again, it is imperative for the process to move beyond the subjective and shift into the objective by creating a larger sense of understanding through an evidence-based approach.

This is where a thorough Evaluation or an in-depth Present Levels of Performance can make a significant difference. For example, with the case above—which also involved a deep-seated attachment issue and fetal alcohol syndrome symptoms—everyone at the table had a different understanding of the student, the disability, and its implications. It's human nature for our past experiences to influence our perceptions of the present. When creating understanding of the student above, a processing-related assessment tool like the WISC and a carefully crafted Functional Behavior Assessment (FBA) allowed the team to go beyond the various opinions and objectively explore how the evidence presented itself.

So many times a review of the WISC cognitive assessment, especially an analysis of the Working Memory and Processing Speed sub-tests, allows us to learn so much more about a student than what is revealed within the full-scale scores themselves. This is essential when a team explores the connection between a student's learning style and their achievement.

- Working Memory: When addressing ADD-related challenges, the initiation, follow-though, and work completion continue to be the focal point of many 504 and IEP team discussions. And the notion of "being willful," "oppositional," and "attention seeking" come up in these conversations all the time. However, when looking at a WISC, especially the Working Memory subtest, it becomes clear that many ADD/ADHD identified students struggle with a processing disorder similar to what one sees in executive functioning related disabilities. As a result, the discussion often moves from an attitude issue to a learning processing challenge. By doing so, parents and students are more likely to join in the discussion, creating a platform leading to mutual understanding.

- Processing Speed: Here again, the data presented in the Processing Speed subtest can help us understand a student when we don't know what's truly going on. For example, many students have sensory-processing or autism-related considerations that often present as anxiety; for these students, slower processing speeds are frequently demonstrated when given a cognitive assessment. This information helps us explore interventions, especially classroom-based accommodations. Many students with processing-speed deficits require instructional scaffolding like visual supports, additional time, and meaning centered/interest-based connections to experience success. If the deficits have gone unnoticed, these students may appear "spaced out," "disinterested," "slow," or "lost in their own thoughts," or "avoiding." Again, when discussing a student's behavior from these descriptions, a defensive position often develops, which is counterproductive to establishing mutual understanding.

Most notably, when behavior is at the core of the issue, it is imperative to truly create an objective understanding of the student, for anything else can appear to be accusatory, and defensive postures can result. So in these situations, a skilled behavior analyst is able to assist the team with the FBA (Functional Behavior Assessment) in reviewing the observations and the data collected. This is another example of how an objective approach supports mutual understanding. Simply put, the purpose of an evidence-based decision model is to help move the conversation from the subjective to an objective point of view with mutual understanding at the core. And with behavior issues, intervention teams need due diligence in making this shift most evident.

One insight I have gained along the advocacy trail is the understanding that if a student brings to school a cluster of inconvenient behaviors, especially if they create a major distraction within the classroom, then the call for IEP intervention takes center stage. In fact, when the level of inconvenience becomes insurmountable for the school, the conversation may also shift to medication. In contrast, when the student is quiet, demure, compliant, and manageable within the classroom, learning disabilities and related intervention may be minimized and presented as developmental and "needing more time to work themselves out" *without* the support of an IEP or 504 Plan. If this is truly a pattern, are we creating a special-needs support system based upon subjective determination of inconvenience? Or are we consistently walking through the response-to-intervention process with an objective frame of reference?

The latter option, an objective approach to decision making, is in everyone's best interest. As long as the Evaluation and the Present Levels of Performance sections of an IEP or 504 Plan are addressed within an evidence-based decision process, highlighting assessment, data, and formalized behavior charting, we all are much better-off. When we take ego, interest, and bias out of

71

the discussion and move toward a data-driven process, we provide everyone a much more comprehensive service through mutual understanding. Now don't get me wrong—I am not suggesting we leave our hearts out of the equation and run the process from a cold perspective; this is far from what I recommend. By opening our hearts to one another, we make connections and create an authentic partnership. However, when the IEP and 504 process moves into the Evaluation or Present Levels of Performance conversations, our collective insights need to be directed by the evidence that presents itself from a thorough assessment of the child, highlighting both strengths and challenges.

Take notice: One of the most transformative tools recommended can be found within the procedural safeguards offered to parents: an Independent Education Evaluation (IEE). Sometimes a fresh pair of eyes makes a difference! When the team feels stuck, the expertise of a clinician from outside the school or district may provide valuable insights. Especially when a log-jam of personal agendas, locked in tried and true ways of thinking fails to do the trick, or when the team feels at wits-end and frustrated by a lack of results. It amazes me how useful this tool can be. At the same time, I am not surprised when I observe reluctance from the staff when an external resource joins the discussion. For most teachers and staff take their work to heart and very personally; they believe their intentions are in the best interest of each student. However, outside consultants have access to an extraordinary number of resources, assessments, and behavior-related tools that may prove to be most helpful within an evidence-based approach to an IEP or 504 Plan team. This is most noticeable when a fresh perspective or newfound information provides the necessary shift in support of mutual understanding. In stressful situations, sometimes people dig in their heels and hold onto ineffective or outdated perceptions. This happens to parents, teachers, and special education directors alike. At times our emotions can get the best of us, as described in Stewart's case:

Stewart was seven years old and in the second grade. Like most boys his age, he enjoyed dogs, video games, and playing in the dirt. By appearance alone, there was nothing unusual about him when you first met him, except you could tell there is a special look in his eyes; Stewart had both charisma and enthusiasm.

I was asked to observe him within his classroom. I was told his behavior was severe; he was described to me by his principal as "the most disturbed kid I have ever seen in all my years … we can't figure him out." As an education advocate, it is always a red flag when a principal makes this point. It's as if somewhere along the way, they stopped trying to appreciate boys like Stewart and instead focus on control, management, and containment rather than understanding. From my perspective, most students act out for good reasons. In Stewart's case, his behavior made absolute sense. Sometimes people don't "get it" because the desire to try to understand may get lost when dealing with an extremely complex kid with very inconvenient behaviors. The foundation of all effective behavior management systems and discipline programs must begin with a clear understanding of the child, first and foremost.

When I entered the classroom, it was impossible to figure out which one was Stewart by observation alone. The whole room— twenty verbally gifted students—were all clamoring for their teacher's attention: calling out answers, freely chatting, and impulsively talking out loud to one another. From what I deciphered within seconds, this first-year teacher's class management skills were nonexistent, and the classroom was out of control. There, sitting closest to the teacher, was Stewart, with his hand up, anxiously waiting to be called upon. It wasn't easy for him to be patient like this, for his brain fired off at lightspeed due to an IQ at the high superior range of 150-plus; his scores placed him within the top 1% of all second graders. "Genius" would be the typical label we used years ago. Now, we call boys like Stewart "complex." He was also diagnosed with ADHD. Nevertheless, everyone on the staff saw Stewart as a troubled young boy who needed to be placed in a special class for emotionally disturbed kids; in fact, the school wanted him to be assessed by a neuropsychologist, for they felt he was "psychotic." Obviously, no one at school took the gifted label seriously, for his behavior was classic within the context of Highly Capable students who are either bored or disengaged. But his parents never gave up. They knew that their son was complex; both gifted and influenced by ADHD / Executive Function; "twice exceptional".

From our point of view, Stewart was acting out due to two factors: poor class management and boredom. The lack of class management triggered Stewart's ADHD tendencies. Often kids with ADHD have difficulty discriminating between auditory and visual stimulation, so chaos and distraction feel like static on a TV set and create internal havoc. For kids like Stewart, when the stimulation hits overload, the ability to self-regulate and self-monitor goes out the window, and impulsivity, distractibility, and anxiety become amped up. On the other hand, Stewart and his ADHD cohorts flourish when guidelines are clearly drawn, classroom routines are predictable and consistently reinforced, and well-designed classrooms replace visual and verbal noise of a traditional classroom. But this was not the case at that time. In fact, it was every student for himself, and Stewart is the type of fellow who would make certain he was the first in everything: first in line, to answer questions, and the first out the door, no matter what. That included pushing, shoving, and calling out—whatever it took, Steward felt the need to be first. . Also, Stewart thrived on hands-on activities where he could build things, draw designs, and create large schemes involving elaborate stories and complex tales. In this classroom, he was asked to do nothing of this sort. In fact, everything was based upon pen-and-paper tasks requiring the second graders to laboriously write at length. The curriculum being implemented did not play to his strengths. It was creating frustration after frustration for him. He was a brilliant young man who needed an expressive outlet, and writing was definitely not his cup of tea. When you are as sharp as Stewart, it is very difficult for the hand to keep up with the mind, and this often created agitation with writing assignments.

As a result, his described "outrageous" behavior was fueled by an out-of-control classroom. Also, class activities failed to tap into his intensely curious nature, for there was nothing in the curriculum that parlayed the enthusiasm and magnetism aligned with his gifts within. Stewart was the type of hands-on kid who could play chess for hours, design extensive sandbox castles, and look through microscopes for days on end.

Nevertheless, nothing like this was offered or considered within Stewart's instructional program.

Typically, a child's behavior is all about cause-and-effect relationships. One of the standard practices with behavior analysis is to determine the causes (antecedents) observed within the acting out and extinguish it by decreasing the variables creating the behavior. Ideally, an effective behavior intervention plan (BIP) would replace disruptive behaviors with new, desired behaviors and create a new effect or desired outcome. Most importantly, behavior is always best understood in light of what's in the child's own perceived best interests. In Stewart's case, as he saw it, it was in his best interests to call out excessively within an out-of-control classroom because he always wanted to be "first." It was also in his best interests, as he saw it, to create his own curriculum by talking about "poopie" and other bathroom-like ideas, for he was perpetually bored with the activities offered in class and he sought the attention of his classmates. In a second-grade classroom, comments about bodily functions and related fluids are universally appreciated by classmates everywhere. Stewart discovered this at an early age; he played to his audience. Nevertheless, this was not appreciated by teachers and staff. In fact, it was so apparent that Stewart felt his teacher did not like him that he overcompensated and deliberately sought the attention of his classmates instead. He performed the daily stand-up routine with the usual poop jokes and was a hit with the eight-year-old crowd.

As an education advocate, I am paid by parents to seek solutions to complex problems involving their child's lack of success in school. In Stewart's case, his parents felt that every time they advocated for their son's needs, they were met by a wall

76

of teachers and administrators who were basically stating two things over and over:

1. *Your child is emotionally disturbed.*

2. *Your parenting skills (or lack of) are the cause of his behavior.*

Both explanations created an adversarial relationship and failed to follow an evidence-based approach.

So I was charged with the responsibility to help the school's intervention team see Stewart in a different light. As I observed, his behavior was not a form of emotional imbalance but was a result of inappropriate class management and ill-advised curriculum. A previously developed FBA and related BIP (behavior plan) highlighted his need for structure, predictability, and appropriate learning, but the team failed to follow this guidance. The cognitive assessment also highlighted a significant discrepancy between his verbal comprehension abilities (at the 150 range) and his working memory skills, identified at the 82nd percentile; this presented an intense challenge for Stewart. After countless meetings, observations, and conversations with the principal, Stewart was finally placed in a new classroom. The teacher was experienced with many tricks and tools of the trade supporting classroom management. Also, this teacher "got" Stewart and appreciated and understood him for who he was—quirks, brilliance, desire to be first, and everything in between. She liked him, and he knew it.

After four weeks in the new classroom, another intervention meeting was called to update parents and staff about Stewart's progress. Within the opening sentence by the principal, we knew

Stewart was experiencing a whole new approach to learning: **success***. The principal simply stated, "I haven't seen Stewart in my office once since we moved him to the new classroom." Consistent with this remark, his teacher offered the following comments, "Stewart looks happy in my class. Sure, he tested the guidelines at first, but when he figured out I meant what I said and that I consistently followed through, he was mine. He has been a great student ever since." Weeks later, Stewart was thriving in a classroom where the following were in evidence:*

- *Consistent guidelines, predictable schedules, and regular reinforcement of behavior.*

- *Engaging instructional activities at each student's instructional and interest level.*

- *And most importantly, a teacher who understands and appreciates his gifts, talents, and quirks. He knows she likes him!*

Months later, I spoke with Stewart's mother. She was overjoyed and described her son "as a completely different kid." For the first time since he entered public school, Stewart was handling school appropriately. Not only was he doing well with his studies, he was making friends, getting along, and enjoying the daily routine without a major event; not once did the principal call home and ask his mom to pick him up. Not only was Stewart appreciated for being Stewart, quirks and all, he was provided a classroom where the overall auditory and visual noise on the outside did not compete with the internal noise within himself. As a result, Stewart was a "different kid." The path from emotionally disturbed to a "great student" was all about finding what Stewart needed and how the system needed to adjust to assure his success.

In this situation, a well-written FBA, related behavior intervention plan, the insights found within a WISC, and solid classroom management made the difference. In contrast to the devastating impact of inconvenience and misunderstanding, an evidence-based approach through observation and behavior analysis trumped control, emotion, and subjectivity.

Sample Evidence Based Evaluation Tools

Academic (cognitive intelligence, processing):

WISC III/IV (Wechsler Intelligence Scale for Children): The standard intelligence test which highlights processing through pattern analysis of the sub-tests; excellent reference complementing additional tests, assessments, and data.

CTONI (Comprehensive Test of Nonverbal Intelligence): An alternative intelligence test with a nonverbal perspective. This test is best for use with students who have language-related issues like autism, speech and language, or ESL.

DAS (Differentiated Ability Scales): This cognitive assessment for kids from 2.5 years old features diagnostic subtests measuring a variety of cognitive abilities including verbal and visual working memory, immediate and delayed recall, visual recognition and matching, processing and naming speed, phonological processing, and understanding of basic number concepts.

Achievement (academic performance):

WIAT/WJR III (Wechsler Individual Achievement Test/Woodcock Johnson): The standard achievement tests featuring achievement in core subjects including reading, math, and written expression. It is broken into sub-tests for each content area.

Kaufman Test of Educational Achievement (KTEA): Covers many of the same criteria within the WIAT and WJR; however, it may take less time.

Behavior:

Connors Continuous Performance Test: An assessment tool addressing attention and related skill sets often associated with ADD/ADHD assessments.

TOVA (Test of Variables of Attention): Another attention-related test administered by schools and within clinical settings.

BASC 2 (Behavior Assessment System for Children): The standard elements include behaviors that are keeping the student from success. Assessment tool addressing a wide range of issues including aggression, antecedents/causes of the behavior, functional purpose of the anxiety, depression, and social skills based upon parent, teacher, and a child's self-assessment.

Language Skills:

CELF (Clinical Evaluation of Language Fundamentals): Another standard evaluation tool highlighting reading, language expression, receptive language, and written language, most notably in the speech and language evaluation process. Excellent tool for higher functioning students with autism or Asperger's syndrome, as well as students with receptive or expressive language concerns. Excellent assessment as a follow-up to WISC or achievement tests.

<u>Physical (balance, coordination, spatial and strength):</u>

Sensory Integration and Praxis Test: This assessment tool given with an IEP would benefit primarily related to sensory, tactile, kinesthetic, and motor-related issues. It is often applied to an OT evaluation, and assists in number of situations, including autism spectrum assessments.

<u>Social, Functional, and Adaptive Life Skills:</u>

Vineland 2 (Vineland Adaptive Behavior Scales): An assessment tool addressing personal and social skills needed for everyday living; helps identify social skills related to intellectual disability or other disorder such as autism, Asperger's syndrome, and developmental delays.

<u>Social and Emotional Development of Infants and Toddlers:</u>

BITSEA (The Brief Infant-Toddler Social and Emotional Assessment): Another standard assessment tool specifically designed for children up to 36 months addressing a wide range of social and emotional skills i.e.; social skills, language, and developmental delays.

Notes:

STRENGTH-BASED INTERVENTION: APPRECIATIVE ADVOCACY

A strength-based approach to IEP or 504 planning takes the intervention process to a higher level by guiding the team toward endless opportunities, an abundance of resources, and innovative interventions. The source of this inspiration comes from a deeper, more enlightened perspective of ourselves and our students: Faith serves as the fundamental guide as part of the practice called *appreciative advocacy*. This approach provides better results than the traditional paradigm highlighting compliance guidelines, resource scarcity, and being limited to "best practices" founded upon fear.

Appreciative advocacy is not new, for it is grounded upon organizational development research called Appreciative Inquiry. Simply, the following insight about Appreciative Inquiry guides this process: "[Appreciative Inquiry] deliberately seeks to discover people's exceptionality—their unique gifts, strengths, and qualities. It actively searches and recognizes people for their specialties—their essential contributions and achievements. And it is based on principles of equality of voice—everyone is asked to speak about their vision of the true, the good, and the possible.

Appreciative Inquiry builds momentum and success because it believes in people. It is an invitation to a positive revolution. Its goal is to discover in all human beings the exceptional and the essential. Its goal is to create organizations that are in full voice!" [Cooperrider, D.L.]

In addition, the principles of appreciative advocacy originate from the belief that all children are a gift waiting to unfold, and this unveiling is part of a process much bigger than what a standards-based curriculum can provide. The overarching theme lies within a faith-based approach to life that suggests we are part of a larger mosaic, and our contributions reflect a grand scheme highlighting purpose and possibility as part of this design. Fundamentally, four universal beliefs take form within appreciative advocacy, each common to major world religions and fundamental to global spiritual practices:

- **Understanding that there is an energy, a presence, or a source unifying each one of us.**

- **Faith in one another and the understanding that we can achieve much more as a group than as an individual.**

- **Belief that we are all an integral part of a larger mosaic-like puzzle, one in which we all influence one another and present a unique gift within this experience called "life."**

- **Knowing our attitudes shape our perceptions; we see what we believe. For example:**

84

o *"What you expect is what you find."* (Aristotle)

o *"Be transformed by the renewing of your mind."* (Apostle Paul)

o *"We are what we think. ... All that we are, arises with our thoughts. With our thoughts we make our world."* (Buddha)

Through a strength-based appreciative advocacy practice, whether guided by IEP or 504 Plan interventions, the starting point will always be from a position of strength rather than weakness. Fundamentally, this is where this book provides a different mindset compared to that often found in traditional Special Education models. Traditionally, we often see our special-needs students as though something is broken, and we focus on the *half-empty* aspects of the situation rather than *half-full.* This belief system, focusing on weakness, is reinforced by parents who believe their children need to be fixed and are desperately trying to find the magic potion to cure their child. Finally, district staff members often face the same challenges with a common belief that resources are limited and their hands are tied due to financial scarcity. It's time for an attitude shift of major proportions.

Also, conventional intervention models limit themselves to "research-based" approaches. Don't get me wrong; I believe best-practice instructional strategies are important considerations for every team to explore. Nevertheless, I have seen too many intervention plans, notably innovation, lost within a cookie-cutter research-based formula. For one-size-fits-all approaches fail to meet the needs of each child when you take in account individuality, uniqueness, and varying learning styles. In contrast, as proposed within this book, the starting point for appreciative advocacy begins with the student and builds upon their success and a genuine sense of promise and potential, which are so important within the intervention process.

Specifically, through IEP or 504 intervention, efforts should always establish an understanding of "what works" rather than focusing exclusively on what is broken. By doing so, the team should be guided by the following inquiry questions:

- **What works best for this student? (Both at home and at school.)**

- **How is promise or potential demonstrated within the evidence and what we know?**

- **What resources are available which support our collaborative efforts as a team?**

- **How do creativity and innovation present themselves in this situation?**

- **As a result of the above, how can we best support this student?**

- **How can we measure our efforts in support of the student's success?**

An excellent demonstration of "What works?" may be best illustrated during one of the most of intense and successful moments in recent U.S. history: the legendary *Apollo 13* space flight. Astronaut James Lovell made the famous comment, "*Houston, we have a problem!*" as he realized the mission was heading toward a catastrophic ending. The flight director, Gene Kranz, responded to the crisis by stating, "*I need to know what is still working.*" He intuitively knew that a position of strength provides a more inspired position in the decision process, and he knew his team needed to tap into innovation and extraordinary creativity under very trying times. This idea holds true in the IEP and 504 process. By highlighting what is working, the team establishes a launching point for creative and inventive discussion, which ultimately supports each child's learning through intervention. Within a very complex and often challenging process, a strength-based conversation guides both 504 and IEP meetings toward an uplifting perspective, because attitude remains the one thing in life that we do have control over.

In our life, we meet a number of people who leave an indelible mark within our memories. There's something extraordinary about these people; often, they bring with them a life-long lesson. Jen and Pat, two parents with a couple of kids on the autism spectrum, always come to mind when I think about building upon "what works." I am forever in gratitude and appreciation for the impact these parents presented in my life as an advocate.

I was contacted by Jen to join their IEP meetings, for there was a gap between home and school in terms of "mutual understanding." District and school staff were not grasping the big picture

87

related to Jen's daughter's disability and her daily performance in school; there was a tendency for the team to see her through the highly inconvenient lens. Also, the intervention tool kit applied by the team didn't align with the diagnosis; it resembled more of a behavior management approach common to classic reinforcement theory with positive and negative consequences in response to actions. So it was Jen's intention to help the team:

1. *Understand her daughter and create a better sense of her diagnosis and establish success-based interventions, and*

2. *Do so from a position of what already works outside of school, for her daughter was doing quite well both in therapeutic settings and social community activities.*

As a demonstration of appreciative advocacy, Jen skillfully set the stage for a collaborative discussion in a way I'll never forget. Before the meeting, Jen and her husband, Pat, prepared fresh baked goods for the team. Though the staff were waiting with apprehension, the tension in the room immediately lifted when we arrived. The smell of oven-fresh chocolate chip cookies established a completely different mindset across the table. Smiles and laughter immediately were shared as everyone shifted from a defensive posture to a family-like greeting as childhood memories and the association of yummy fresh-baked goodies took center stage within the room.

Building upon the shift in the room's energy, immediately following introductions Jen placed a photograph of her daughter on the table—a large 8x10 professionally shot photograph that was no less than stunning. She opened up with the following statement: "For those of you who don't know my daughter, she is a remarkable young girl ... " and then told the team in less than a minute the extraordinary nature of her daughter, including her interests, strengths, and a long-range vision of her daughter's promise and potential. Then, she stated her objectives for the meeting: "I want us to develop the best IEP possible for my daughter in support of her success at school." And then the meeting began. Successfully!

At the *Institute of HeartMath,* one of the premier science-based research programs addressing emotional wellness and peak performance, calls this shift a classic application of "Freeze Frame". This technique supports emotional balance, calming strategies, and heart-based decision making within individuals and also within groups. The process strives for a change of heart amongst decision makers, helping people move from an emotionally rigid position—whether defensive, close-minded, or tense—to a lighter attitude lifted by gratitude, appreciation, and positive emotions. The process becomes collaborative and guided not only by the head but also with a true change of heart. The new way of working with the team includes participants' emotions and supports creativity, partnership, and innovative thinking. By establishing a framework based upon appreciation and promise, a genuine shift unfolds. In contrast, stress and tension steal this opportunity from the process. This is the true nature of appreciative advocacy at work.

Appreciative Advocacy: ADD/ADHD

The ADD intervention process needs to address the following themes: processing, social relationships, and the need to support learning through the student's interests. These are all strengths often presented by students with ADHD.

Within our classrooms, students with ADD/ADHD continue to present some of the greatest challenges facing teachers today. Once again, if we create opportunities for success from a strength-based position, these kids can be the true movers and shakers in the classroom, school, and in life itself. One of the best definitions of the ADD/ADHD condition is described in Thom Hartmann's *Complete Guide to ADHD*. Hartmann compares ADD/ADHD to the hunter's mindset (always on the hunt; scanning) in contrast to living in a farmer's world (waiting for things to harvest; patient). This is most important to consider in school, where we emphasize the farmer's mindset exclusively: sitting in chairs, performing paper and pencil tasks, and having limited opportunities for movement. After working with hundreds of kids with this diagnosis, I see it like this: ADD/ADHD is the "enthusiastic child" in a constant state of search and discovery, who can also be described as the "energetic child" in a constant state of search and destroy. It's a matter of attitude. As we shift our perspective, we can build on the strengths and support each child through appropriate intervention.

There are times when a condition like ADD/ADHD may appear to be a disorder, like in school, but in other situations, the traits of ADD/ADHD are a blessing or a gift. For example, when I'm on an airplane, I'm hoping there are air traffic controllers with ADD in the tower, for it is imperative for these people to continuously scan their monitors without locking onto any one flight for too long. Also, I appreciate the controllers' ability to multitask in these tension-filled moments, for people with ADD often demonstrate extraordinary rapid-fire decision making skills that lend themselves well to a crisis situation. I can rest easy knowing there is an abundance of ADD in the control tower. Also, when I go to a nice restaurant, I hope that the maître d' or hostess also demonstrates the gift of ADD. I benefit when the person running the reservation side of the restaurant regularly scans the diners for open tables and demonstrates an understanding of timing within the room instead of focusing on the details of what each patron is being served or drinking. We can leave the latter level of focus to the waiters!

One of the most common characteristics of people with ADHD is the ability to demonstrate enthusiasm for everything. Life appears to be a wealth of wonderful opportunities for these kids. Within a team setting, I love having someone on board with unbridled passion. Some of our most inspirational leaders, our true innovators, may have had ADD/ADHD: Walt Disney, Albert Einstein, Frank Lloyd Wright, and Emily Dickenson, to name a few. Also, an extraordinary level of compassion and empathy for others is a well-documented characteristic in many people with ADD/ADHD. Within the classroom, kids with ADD/ADHD are often more aware and concerned about what others are doing than their own work. I cannot imagine life without these people. Enthusiasm is contagious!

Nevertheless, within the classroom, where we are expecting students to sit in chairs for endless hours and work primarily with writing-based activities, these kids may be seen as incredibly inconvenient when their extraordinary gifts are not tapped appropriately. No matter how much medication you distribute, when you have a student with an abundance of life within, like a Robin Williams or Jim Carey, you truly cannot contain this level of energy within the typical classroom. When channeled appropriately, these kids are a blast. When they're not directed, these kids can be a bust. So once again, it's a matter of how we see these kids first and foremost. Everything else then falls into place.

Years ago, as I made the transition from an administrator to an advocate, I returned to the classroom part-time and taught a number of classes, including both Gifted and General Education. It provided an extraordinary foundation for my future work. In fact, I returned to the classroom one more time in 2015, as I will describe later in this book, and discovered an astounding set of insights and understandings about teaching, students, and learning which would have never been available if I hadn't taken this opportunity. Due to my classroom experiences, I can honestly say I understand the whole notion of "blast or bust."

Envision a classroom with 34 students, and 19 are identified with either IEP or 504 Plan support, highlighting ADD as the leading diagnosis within the mix. Also, imagine the same classroom with 20 high-energy fifth grade boys and 14 girls including a "free and reduced lunch count" at 60-70% of the class. This class was a lively bunch. So I had to figure out what worked pretty quickly, or I would have been overwhelmed by the development of an ADHD circus!

I figured out there needed to be outlets for the abundant level of energy and enthusiasm. So I began including hands-on art activities related to the core lessons, extended recess periods, and ample opportunities for cooperative group activities. These kids loved to hang out with one another and endlessly talk if guidelines weren't provided. I could have lost control of this class within a moment's notice. In fact, on numerous occasions, I did. I clearly remember one day I stepped out of the classroom for a few seconds while a student teacher was running the class. Within minutes, the police department showed up at my doorstep. An anonymous 911 call had come from my classroom phone. I later discovered that a conversation about 911 within an earlier health class had evolved into a game of "dare" as I stepped out to make necessary copies. And within seconds, the classroom chatter went from "dare" to one of the boys taking this as a golden moment to prove himself by showing everyone he was up for the challenge. So he dialed 911 while I stepped out. This was that kind of class! You never knew what to expect at any given moment, for the fine line between "blast or bust" was always demonstrated, especially as classic ADD characteristics of the classroom were well represented throughout the student body.

One day I took this class on a field trip. I took special precautions to assure we hit the prerequisite ADD benchmarks: Expend energy in the AM, present socializing in the early afternoon, close the day out with quiet, and provide more reflective hands-on arts-related activities in the late afternoon. In fact, this ended up one of the best days anyone ever had! Here's how it went:

During the bus ride, I rewarded kids with "raffle tickets" as the guidelines were clearly stated:

- *Sit in your assigned seat throughout the whole bus ride.*

- *Talk so your friends nearby could hear you, but not the whole bus.*

- *Keep your hands to yourself.*

And everyone who met these simple guidelines received raffle tickets toward the weekly candy bar drawing at the end of the week. Everyone received tickets when the ride to our first activity was uneventful.

Our first stop was an indoor fitness studio where the kids could get physical for a couple hours, traversing ropes, and applying extensive hand and foott holds on a climbing wall. They loved it.

We then followed this with a visit to a local park for our lunch session. As I recall the day almost twenty years later, I vaguely remember this as one of the most relaxing lunch hours I ever experienced with any group of students. Everyone was calm and relaxed, and the previous experience with the climbing walls caused everyone to feel both exhausted and invigorated at the same time.

So when we finally made it to our most important destination, a local museum highlighting a snowboarding exhibit (aligned with our study of state geography), our kids were ready for the task at hand. This exhibit was sponsored by a local snowboarding company. As a result, guests were invited to create their own boards and submit their designs to the company through the museum docent program.

Once again, I was stunned by the kids, for they embraced the exhibit and the activities with full attention and cooperation. Crayons, marking pens, and colored pencils were shared back and forth amongst the students while they created their own designs, whether in pairs or individually. In fact, what impressed me the most was the art docent's final comments as we packed for our bus trip back to school: "We have seen hundreds of students and many classes throughout this exhibit, but never have we seen such a good group of kids; they are so quiet and focused. Are these kids from your gifted program?" I smiled and actually caught myself laughing as she said this. If she only knew! But then again, she had it right. These were gifted kids; they just weren't placed in the traditional Highly Capable program. They were creative, engaged, and motivated. They also received on this day what they craved: a physical outlet, interest-based learning, and an opportunity to create. I had never been more proud of a group of students as I was this day; clearly, this field trip was a blast!

Most ADD/ADHD students receive support through the "health impairment" category, which does not require the need for a WISC Abilities Assessment within the evaluation. A well written, strength-based IEP/504 Plan supporting the needs of an ADD/ADHD student should also include data found within a WISC or WJR cognitive assessment. The evidence within amplifies the processing capabilities of the student. Though most ADD/ADHD students demonstrate strengths in processing speed (the ability to cognitively connect the information through speed) and a relative weakness in working memory (the amount of information one can take in at one time), this is not always the case. Each student provides a unique profile as measured by the evidence.

When empathy and compassion are at the core of the personality of a typical student with ADD/ADHD, a well-written IEP/504 Plan incorporates the student's social attributes as well, for relationships are often critical considerations for these students. I cannot begin to tell you how many cases I have worked where the success of the student with ADD/ADHD is solely based upon the relationship between the student and their teacher, and everyone's feelings are delicate in these matters. No matter how well-written an IEP or a 504 Plan is, if the student feels unliked or not connected to the teacher, the whole process may hit the wall. For Stewart, his relationship to his second teacher was the glue holding everything together. And in the case of the first teacher, the strained relationship was the toxic chemistry tearing it all apart.

Furthermore, a strength-based IEP or 504 Plan will often incorporate an ADD/ADHD-diagnosed student's interests within the accommodation/specially designed instruction plan. Many of these kids are all about enthusiasm and passion. If a team fails to make this connection, then you may be facing an uphill battle all along the way. Kids with ADD/ADHD are often more inspired and moved by their internal callings than they are by rewards from others. Though they may want to please, many are guided by the gifts and talents within. For example, once Lauren was released from the traditional curriculum and supported by a vocational career path through cosmetology and fashion, she literally evolved into a whole new person like a caterpillar turning into a butterfly!

In a nutshell, the learning disabilities associated with this ADD/ADHD are often subtle, especially when they impact visual or auditory processing skills within reading, note-taking, listening, or writing. In contrast, actions or behavior may not be so understated. Often these students are perceived as "willfully lacking self-control" or needing "more parental guidance," all while support and related services are difficult to acquire. As a result, ADD/ADHD or any other processing-oriented disability is not easily detected without an in-depth evaluation. When we follow an evidence-based approach to understanding, our students with ADD/ADHD often require finely tuned organization and planning accommodations (processing related), social connection with adults and peers, a well-designed behavior plan, and a positive prognosis in support of the challenges and gifts found within. Take the story of Lucas, for example.

I ran into Lucas at the local supermarket after a long spell without us seeing one another. When you live in a small town like I did, especially if you were an elementary principal, you take notice of kids as they grow up through the years. What caught my attention the most was that standing before me in the frozen food section was a living example of a true role model—a hero. I heard through the grapevine that Lucas performed two tours of duty in Iraq and returned home uncertain of his future: a third deployment in Iraq, applying for college, or a different path altogether. All I knew was that the young man I was talking to demonstrated an extraordinary level of self-confidence way beyond that of his peers.

Years ago, when I first met Lucas, he was a regular in the principal's office. He was one of those kids who spent endless hours under my supervision, for he was always in trouble of some kind; Lucas had ADHD and dyslexia—a double dose of learning disability. As a sixth grader, he was constantly aggravated by the fact that he could not read like his peers. As he progressed through the school system without support, the challenges of reading increased, and so did his frustration. He was a teacher's nightmare. He was not only intelligent (hands-on/ visual spatial smart; the type of student who required something in his hands at all times to remain focused) but also very confrontational and unwilling to put up with anything that seemed unfair or unjust. If he didn't like something or didn't want to do the activity, he would speak his mind. Between my office and recess, he was frequently out of the classroom. Recess was another story in itself.

Since finding the gifts within and building upon strengths is at the core of true advocacy, it may have been difficult identifying

98

Lucas's gifts and blessings within the typical school setting. He was unsuccessful in the regular classroom. It was at recess where we started to discover his true calling. Unlike others who got into fights for selfish purposes and bully-like tendencies, Lucas was the recess guardian, protecting the less-fortunate students and those who were tormented and easily picked-on. Since I was the principal, these actions at recess caught my attention. It made absolute sense that he would one day join the military and unselfishly serve and protect others through the National Guard.

After Lucas left the elementary program, I was aware of the trials and pitfalls that continued to haunt him throughout middle school. As with most students with ADHD, he found that his school experience was a "square peg in a round hole" mismatch. For Lucas, the breadth of his school experience was all about failure. He was on the path toward truancy and early dropout until one summer when his life truly turned around due to an unforeseeable event.

After another school year of suspensions and failing classes, it was agreed that Lucas would be better off staying with his father on family property in another state. He would be able to work off his excess energy with ample acreage all about and forget about school for a while. No one imagined that his daily swim in the local creek would lead to major life changes. Apparently, one day Lucas jumped in head first and hit bottom, fracturing his spine. As a result, he was immediately fitted with a spinal injury device restricting all movement for a minimum of six months. Nevertheless, one of the few movements he was able to perform was a physical maneuver similar to rowing.

Following extensive therapy, Lucas continued to perform endless hours of rowing. It was his passion during recovery. Throughout the healing process, Lucas's parents explored every avenue imaginable for school options. It was later determined that he would attend a school in Canada with a nationally recognized rowing team and an exemplary success rate working with students with learning disabilities. Due to his alternative high school program, Lucas experienced extraordinary success both academically and socially. In fact, he earned a spot on the Canadian Junior Olympic Rowing team.

Lucas is truly a role model. When we reconnected in the frozen foods section, he told me he was serving his community as an emergency medical technician (EMT). His gift of service found a remarkable outlet that back in grade school, on the recess playground, was cause of suspension and discipline. In addition, Lucas also mentored local athletes as the head coach of the junior rowing club. Clearly, he was giving back to a sport which in many ways saved his life. Who would imagine that a tragic diving accident would lead to such an extraordinary path?

Processing disabilities, often associated with ADD/ADHD, are most difficult to detect, for they often are masked and compensated for in other ways. These disabilities may be lost in the shuffle of inconvenient, impulsive behavior or related disciplinary measures. As our children's advocates, our greatest responsibility and challenge is to seek and discover the gifts within, for they lead us toward a better understanding of our students and their path. In light of Lucas's story, one could say it was a leap of faith that lead to his true potential.

100

Appreciative Advocacy: Autism Spectrum

Consistent within appreciative advocacy, the intervention process for students on the autism spectrum requires a detective-like sense of discovery in creating a strength-based IEP or 504 Plan. Due to the nature of autism, the unfolding of someone's gifts, talents, and strengths may require a more in-depth understanding by the intervention team. Now more than ever, we are seeing increasing numbers of students diagnosed with autism, and at the same time, the definition of the spectrum and related symptomatic behaviors appears to be expanding as well. In fact, back in 1983, 1 in 10,000 students were diagnosed with autism. In 2000, 1 in 188 students were diagnosed on the spectrum. One in 88 in 2008, and now, as this is written, 1 in 65 children are diagnosed with autism. As a result, the intervention process requires us to work with an alarming number of students demonstrating a highly complex set conditions and behaviors. Teachers, staff, and administrators are required to be innovative with their limited resources in support of these kids, but most importantly, IEP and 504 intervention teams are called upon to reach beyond their comfort zones in creating innovative, appropriate, and effective interventions. Autism presents the most challenging set of kids I have ever worked with.

From my perspective, autism is not a disease, nor is it a condition requiring a cure. As I see it, autism is a part of life—a sensory response by highly sensitive individuals who have an extraordinary gift of empathy (sensitivity) and sensory perception that may require intensive therapy (social—expressive language—sensory). It also requires parents, teachers, and other loved ones to extend themselves to new levels of appreciation, love, and understanding. Furthermore, I do not believe that autism is caused by vaccinations. Nevertheless, the invasive impact of the medications often presents extreme symptoms by kids on the spectrum due to the intensity of their sensory response. This hypersensitivity is also observed with diet and nutrition. Due to their sensitive nature, these children may also react badly to the foods they eat. Food coloring, preservatives, and chemicals found within the soil often trigger inflammatory responses in kids who are on the spectrum. Furthermore, due to an intense/acute level of sensory perception and inflammatory responses, many kids 1-3 years old who are diagnosed with autism shut down and close themselves off, especially as they're beginning to acclimatize to the world outside themselves.

Typical developmental growth patterns of infants and toddlers are founded upon interaction with their environments at this age, making this age a crucial and profound one. These highly sensitive children, later to be identified on the spectrum, shut themselves off from their environment due to the intensity of their sensory and inflammatory responses. Flight or fight response patterns are part of human nature when we experience stress, anxiety, and a general feeling of being overwhelmed, emotionally and physically.

For the record, I don't believe children with autism truly shut down, nor are they cognitively/emotionally in a coma-like state. Developmentally, many of the kids I have met are intellectually focused, and they direct their cognitive abilities toward repetitive activities and familiar settings because they seek the soothing and comforting nature of structure, patterns, and repetition. These initial learning patterns often touch upon innate gifts, talents, and learning styles. The inconvenient aspect of this behavior pattern is best described as an unwillingness to accept change or an adverse response to transitions. Obviously, these behaviors do not create "Kodak moments" within the family photo album; in fact, an autism diagnosis can create a serious level of tension within the family structure.

Also, as a result of limited social-language development at the critical ages of 1-3 years old, a child's skill development in social receptive/expressive language may be impaired. Though the deficiency may appear significant when compared to that of a typically developing child, social/language skill development follows a continuum. Such development likely stays the course, but it has a unique timeframe—many kids on the spectrum establish their own developmental timeline, and they require therapeutic support, direct instruction, patience, and understanding along the way. These kids are remarkable young people who shape the environments around them in ways beyond what conventional wisdom assumes they should be doing. They require outside-of-the-box understanding when their developmental pattern is not traditional.

One of the most fascinating elements of the autism experience, from my perspective, is how early on the gift seems to present itself. With a typical developing child, we often begin to see natural talents evolve prior to the preadolescent period, 9-11 years old. Then again, many on the spectrum appear to exhibit gifts, talents, and highly focused interests as early as 2-3 years of age. From a teaching perspective, the following observation and insights are important considerations:

- High interest focus/obsessive-compulsion interests provide comfort zones for our kids on the spectrum due to the hyper-anxiety associated with sensory overload. Though a four-year-old may obsess over *Thomas the Train,* he or she won't necessarily grow up to be a conductor, but there are processing tendencies and talents that may be found within this obsession. Most importantly, we need to spend time observing and watching for patterns rather than passing judgment about how strange or bizarre these compulsive interests may be. Ironically, when a typically developing adult demonstrates a similar set of compulsive behaviors associated with sports teams or cats, it's called a "passion" rather than a condition requiring a diagnosis!

- Also, due to the nature of social skill development, often children on the spectrum are not easily influenced by compliance; many don't have a desire to seek adult affirmation within the typical developmental pattern. As a result, many kids on the autism spectrum take to their own internal motivation, inspiration, and talents, rather than responding to those presented by their parents and teachers. This is why an effective instructional intervention plan builds upon a student's interests. If this is not the case, these kids may interpret reward systems as forms of manipulation and respond with greater intensity through defiance.

Absolutely, the autism spectrum experience puts families, parents, and schools in an extraordinary state of inconvenience. It may feel like playing a lifelong puzzle, guessing what works and what doesn't through endless hours of trial and error. Sometimes it takes years to finally get it right. Nevertheless, autism is often described as a sensory condition as well as a disorder significantly impacting the learning process, for anxiety is a common theme for most kids on the spectrum. So the best we can do for kids on the spectrum from an appreciative advocacy perspective is to decrease anxiety.

Decreasing Anxiety in Children on the Autism Spectrum

- With the support of experts in the field, establish a clearly designed sensory profile to minimize the level of sensory distractions and build upon strengths in light of learning styles and successful learning modalities. This is another example of how the WISC can play an important part of the initial evaluation, for processing is a critical component of understanding a student's learning style. Also, the support of an outside consultant for sensory-related assessment will be a valuable resource, for a well-written sensory profile will continue to be an area of great need throughout the school experience of a child with autism.

- Identify successful social communication relationships outside of school and build from there; acknowledge what works. Expressive and receptive language will most likely be an ongoing area of focus. For example, if a preadolescent student tends to gravitate toward younger peers for social relationships, atypical for their grade-level peers, the IEP or 504 Plan would best serve the student by arranging social connections with younger students as part of the school day as a tutor or recess buddy.

- Create bridges in learning between interests and school-based curriculum as needed; if a student is into trains, for example, extend learning into trains as much as possible. Differentiated learning through project-based activities has been used in gifted education for years and needs to be applied here as well. *Virginia Department of Education, Office of Special Education and Student Services*

Years ago, I was introduced to James. He had a warm smile, a friendly face, and a jovial presence, like a twenty-something Santa Claus without the beard and the red suit. He left an impression that has been with me ever since. I was scheduled as the guest speaker at a local autism support group meeting, and James was the first to arrive. Initially, I thought he was a member of the hospital staff setting up the room. He moved around the place as if he were familiar with the surroundings: setting up chairs, moving things about in place, being mindful. Then as we went around the room with our introductions, I was surprised to find out that James was a twenty-four-year-old with Asperger's. And he attended these sessions each month and had been loyally doing so for almost two years. Though my prepared presentation never took place because only a small group of five showed up that evening, James and I exchanged stories, resources, and laughter for an hour or so before we called it an early evening. Looking back, I walked away with way more than I imagined, for I had met James.

When James was in public school, he was "odd," "the geek," "the special needs kid." He probably heard a hundred other disparaging nicknames that described everything but the wonderful person he is today. He told us how he was first diagnosed with ADHD, then as bipolar, then clinically depressed ("I wasn't depressed, I just didn't want to be with people ... that really pissed me off when I heard that"), then finally, at the age of twenty-one, he was diagnosed with Asperger's Syndrome. As he stated, "Finally, someone could explain to me what was going on inside ... I felt relieved to know why I am the way I am." Clearly, James had evolved to where he was truly becoming comfortable with himself and how he fit in the world. An affirming diagnosis set him in the right direction.

As he was described his new part-time job, one where he could use one of his talents—exemplary eye-hand coordination—I got the clear impression he was content. He was able to contribute and be a part of our world, the one in which most of us go to work each day, earn a paycheck, and if we're lucky enough, we know we have made a difference along the way. Knowing we have an impact helps us sleep at night and most importantly, provides the inspiration to wake up each day. For James, this motivation came in the form of fixing labeling guns for retail stores. With great detail and enthusiasm, he described the process at work and the different types of guns used across the country. He proudly expressed how easy it was for him to diagnose the broken guns and solve the problems. His employer was wise enough to identify James's skills during the interview for a custodial position. When James was asked about his interests, he went on a long-winded explanation about Legos, Transformers, and other collectable gadgets. In James's words: "The interview was horrible. I could not answer any of the questions correctly. I was way too nervous. But once I was able to talk about stuff I like, it went well." So well that they immediately figured out they had the perfect guy for a different job—they needed someone who loved to figure out how small things work, like broken labeling guns. In retrospect, his dedication to the job made a profound impression on me. We can all learn from James. It's not about the grand scale in which we contribute to the world. Not everyone can be president, a rock star, or a rocket scientist. It's in the mindfulness and attention to detail that we can make a difference, especially when we are doing something we are good at.

Dr. Martin Luther King Jr. said it best while addressing a group of middle school age students: "If it falls upon your lot to be a street sweeper, sweep streets like Michelangelo painted pictures, sweep streets like Beethoven composed music ... Sweep streets so well that all the hosts of heaven and earth will have to pause and say: Here lived a great street sweeper who swept his job well." James exemplifies exactly what Dr. King was describing. James fixed labeling guns like a surgeon performs heart surgery, with precision and intuition. I was moved and touched by James's presence. Through his example, he taught me more than

I ever imagined that evening. This was the first of many experiences that helped me develop the philosophy behind appreciative advocacy. It was pure intuitive intelligence of the interviewer to ask James a question about what he liked to do after the interview moved from bad to worse. It was sheer genius to see the gift within. James provided an exemplary instance of appreciative advocacy at work—building upon strength, for he is truly an exceptional employee and an individual of character.

Appreciative Advocacy: Learning Disabilities: Writing, Reading, Math, Organization, and Behavior

Within a strength-based IEP or 504 Plan, we are choosing to flow downstream rather than rowing upstream as we develop interventions. It's a matter of identifying the strategies, accommodations, and specially designed instructional techniques that yield the greatest gain based upon what already works. The following ideas are offered as possible interventions for common categories requiring support.

Writing: I attend countless meetings in which the disability and intervention focus falls within the skillset identified as *written expression.* Many of our students struggle with pen-and-paper tasks. At the same time, these kids are actively engaged in gaming activities and computer-based interactive entertainment as well as texting and emailing friends. They're certainly using written expression outside the classroom. So why not use word processing and computers as part of the intervention plan instead of the traditional pen and paper? Typically, students who struggle with dysgraphia and writing with pen and pencil are more apt to work at writing challenges through technology. I know this sounds obvious in the twenty-first century, but we are still requiring these kids to use nineteenth century tools, and we've met with little success. For example, when faced with writing assignments, the following strategies do work. Over time, the reluctant writer begins to take on the writing process as an effective communication tool.

Conversational Expression: Engaging students in a conversation related to the writing prompt or topic gets the ball rolling, especially for students who struggle with initiation, processing, organization and planning, and idea development. As the conversation moves forward, the teacher or peer utilizes one- to three-word phrases within graphic organizers to encapsulate the key concepts. This may require specially designed instruction through an IEP to establish the conversational setting before or after the assignments are distributed within the General Education setting. This type of "front loading" or "back filling," through conversation, is an essential part of the prewriting process.

Graphic Organizers: Once the graphic organizers are embedded within instruction and the student is able to transition into independence with short phrases via these visual tools, the writing process takes shape. It is best to keep things at this level rather than pushing the whole enchilada (like sentences, paragraphs, and essays). There are many graphic organizer tools online as well for students who are tech geeks.

Sentences: As the phrases are well established within the graphic organizer stage, building well- written sentences is the next step. This includes teaching the following concepts: subject/predicate relationships, adverbs, adjectives, and creating voice within these short forms of writing. I believe we need to teach how to walk effectively before we can expect students to run. The writing process builds methodically upon strengths rather than weaknesses. Poetry provides an exemplary form of expression, one with more flexibility and ease for students who struggle with traditional writing. Again, it's best to initially create a purpose for writing rather than pushing a five-paragraph essay as the only option.

Paragraphs and Essays: Finally, once the writing process has established itself with a wider skill base, including meaningful topics and interest-based writing, the sentences naturally evolve into paragraphs and essays. Too often the writing process for special-needs students creates frustration for so many, it's all about "not meeting standard". As a result, the students pick up on this. An intentional approach, one step at a time, tends to yield the greatest results over the long haul.

Reading: Here again, the basis for all intervention is founded upon an evaluation-based decision intervention model. Most reading disabilities focus on three modalities: *Sound/Symbol Recognition* (processing), *Sight Word Vocabulary* (working memory), and *Comprehension/ Meaning* (processing and cognitive reasoning). Fluency may also be addressed. Here's where the WISC and related reading skill inventories work in tandem to determine the best intervention for a student.

When the conversation about an IEP or 504 process is limited to the specific curriculum or instructional tools and methodology by grade level, we tend to experience the challenge of pushing square pegs into round holes. I am suggesting that the best intervention process is solely based upon the evidence demonstrated through assessment and evaluation, rather than school-based curriculum alone. For example, some students excel at sight word vocabulary because their working memory is extraordinary, but due to the slow process of "sounding out words," they feel like failures at reading. These kids often do best when they build upon their strengths and establish a wider base of sight words. Research supports vocabulary development as one of the essential links between poverty and reading disabilities. Due to the contrast between the assessed vocabulary between second-grade students coming from higher social demographic backgrounds (up to 8,000 root words) compared to students entering second grade from impoverished homes (as low as 4,000 root words), this discrepancy often remains the sole difference between success and failure throughout school.

As a result, effective reading instruction incorporates a rich vocabulary component prior to reading comprehension activities as a "front load" strategy in support of meaning development. Also, some students comprehend reading with skill and acuity but suffer with fluency because their ability to process the parts (sound symbol recognition) takes away from the whole (meaning). This is best demonstrated when you compare student achievement with a DIBELS fluency assessment, in conjunction with a Cloze reading test [omitted word assessment], which leaves out key words and assesses comprehension. Overall, instead of advocating for a specific reading strategy for all students who struggle, I support designing reading programs based upon what works for each specific child, and then building upon success as well as interest levels. An evidence-based approach to reading intervention yields greater success than a global approach highlighting general "best practices" and specific school/district curriculum across all grade levels. Appreciative advocacy guides the IEP or 504 team toward individualized intervention rather than one-size-fits-all formulas.

Math: As with reading, the most effective math intervention is founded upon the students' strengths, learning style, and their processing preferences. For example, some students excel within a hands-on, Montessori-like developmental approach. Unfortunately, there isn't enough time for this approach to develop during the early elementary years since most students are generally pushed beyond the manipulatives to the paper/pencil tasks way too early. Also, other students do best with a formalized, concrete set of algorithms often associated with "drill and kill." Nevertheless, public schools tend to minimize repetition and dismiss rote-learning as lower-level thinking. As a result, kids who excel through memorization of core facts, have been shortchanged the last twenty years. The emphasis within most K–6 programs follows an "investigation" meaning-centered approach. This doesn't work for everyone. Again, the best approach to math instruction and intervention is one that is evidence based, assessment driven from a diagnostic approach, and most importantly, builds upon each student's strengths.

As with written expression, numbers of math students are motivated by technology and computer- assisted learning. As a result, there are many exceptional programs which create a bridge between high interest and students who have struggled with math in the past (due to a disconnect with traditional instructional models). I have personally seen hundreds of students excel at math skill acquisition through computer-assisted learning as well as hands-on / project-based activities. Again, I am not proposing that all students need a technology-supported intervention, but I am suggesting it be considered within an appreciative advocacy lens, which builds upon strengths.

In addition, due to the impact of processing speed and working memory on math acquisition skills, the information within the WISC provides valuable data for math interventions streamlined toward a student's strength. Some students need additional repetitions in initial instruction or more processing time to make the connection. Backfill strategies, where learning is supported by additional teaching after the initial direct instruction, are most valuable for many students with learning disabilities. Also, for those students who may have verbal comprehension strengths, the need to "talk it through" before they tackle complex processes provides an excellent example of "front loading," which can also be a powerful intervention for students. And then there are the visual kinesthetic learners, like the kids who are addicted to Legos and other manipulatives, who need to see math through their own eyes and hands. Here again, this method may be time-restrictive; however, with so many students identified as having visual-spatial strengths, the benefit of developing math instruction based upon real-life experiences (cooking, building, crafting) is quite evident when you see how students connect to math through hands-on engagement.

Math is unique because it fundamentally builds upon learning in a sequential format and often does not traditionally fall within the scope of a student's life experience. In contrast to other areas of the curriculum that may build upon "worldly knowledge" and reading skill development, many students with learning disabilities see math as having no applications in the real world. As a result, the bridges created between instruction, a student's learning style, and real-life application are essential to math skill acquisition. For many students with special needs, math skill development resembles a foreign language and requires a strong diagnostic intervention system to truly understand the appropriate pathway toward success. As stated before, the team needs to ask the question "What works?" first and foremost.

Organization: Back in the 1980s and 90s, very few students qualified for special education or needed organization-related support, either through a 504 Plan or under the services of an IEP. Within today's classrooms, organization and planning or executive functioning often require specially designed instruction, especially for students who qualify with a health impairment through a processing-related disorder or autism. Here again, the best intervention support is one that builds upon a student's strength. For example, if a student demonstrates auditory processing strengths but has challenges with visual processing, one typical accommodation assures that listening comprehension guides the learning process and note-taking takes a backseat during the introduction of new concepts. This strategy may assure the key conceptual ideas are developed before asking the student to focus on the written expression side of learning. Also, for students who are evaluated with visual memory strengths in contrast to auditory processing, the 504 Plan or IEP may best support the student through an accommodation requiring instruction to match visual aids and graphic organization supports on the white board or computer screens in conjunction with verbal directions and instructions. Again, it's all about first aligning the strengths with the student's needs and learning.

Also, one of the greatest challenges facing students with organizational/processing disorders is that their working memory may often be at the center of the deficits. Asking a middle school student to remember assignments from first period and review them during fifth period in a Resource Room setting may be almost impossible. The same goes for students who struggle with homework completion, for the memory gap between instruction during class and study time at home may also be so significant that the student is unable to recognize or remember the details required for work completion. As a result, one of the most important features of organization-based 504 Plans and IEP support is a well-designed communication plan between General Education teachers, Resource Room support, and home, so everyone is on board, working from the same page, and aware of assignments, projects, and long-range due dates. In the business world, people who perform this type of organizational service are called administrative assistants or executive secretaries. No one complains that a CEO is "lazy," "irresponsible," or "needing self-discipline," when they rely on such support staff, yet many students are described in this negative way.

Sarah was a typical teenager. Often, it was difficult to identify the fine line between the impact of one phenomenon, described as "being a teenager," and another, the diagnosis of ADD, which was well documented within her school records. Her grades reflected another story: She was earning C's and D's in all General Education courses, with an A in band, her true love. She was one of those Band Geeks who sang tunes in her head all day and frequently whistled during class. She also had an extraordinary knack for auditory memory. Also, she received an F in her organization class, which was part of her IEP. In further investigation of the situation, there were two incongruent elements of the organization class that needed to be addressed:

First, there was no connection between the General Education assignments and the organization support services; students were not able to spend additional time on assignments even though many of the IEP-supported students struggled with

117

processing-related disorders and needed additional time for work completion. The organization instructor had no idea what the students were doing in their General Education classes. So instead of accessing support with extended time on assignments, Sarah was unable to complete daily assignments, even though the IEP and related evaluation clearly stated that her needs were challenged by processing limitations. She had scored very low on both the Working Memory and the Processing Speed subsections of the WISC, though her verbal comprehension scores were in the "high superior" range.

Second, the organization class was founded upon a study skills curriculum and was run like a typical class requiring the students to learn organizational skills with chapters, tests, and exams. For many of the students like Sarah, not only was the content incredibly uninteresting, but it failed to serve their needs; it was one more requirement with which they struggled. It was ironic that Sarah was seeing an after-school tutor to help her complete her IEP-based organization class assignments. As a result, Sarah had to let something go to keep up with her classes.

By the time Sarah's parents contacted me, their daughter was feeling like a complete failure in school. Though she was barely passing with C's and D's, she already had "checked-out" by February of the school year. Her attendance patterns demonstrated frequent tardiness in all classes except Band. So we began to figure out what makes Sarah tick and how to support her academic success in school.

It did not surprise me that most teachers were on the same page when it came to describing Sarah within their classrooms: Good natured, hard-working, social to the point of being a bit distracting. Everyone laughed about her insistent whistling and singing during class time. They also stated that she failed to complete assignments, especially homework. After further inquiry, it was apparent that only one class reflected Sarah's potential: Band. So we explored various accommodations and interventions that aligned with her gifts and talents instead of continuing down the same path of missing assignments and incomplete projects.

One of the changes made for Sarah was to immediately drop the organization class and replace with a Resource Room Study Hall setting. Sarah did not need additional curriculum thrown in front of her. What she needed, like many kids with organization and planning challenges need, was additional time to process the content presented in class. In Sarah's case, once we got things in order, she was encouraged to listen to the class lectures and instruction without the distraction of notetaking, for her auditory memory was amazing. A set of teacher or student notes was provided as an accommodation. This was also supported by a small recording device which provided a second or third listening session of the initial instruction. Also, the IEP was rewritten to include accommodations requiring teachers to review Sarah's daily planner for accuracy, legibility, and required signatures from all classes to assure everyone was monitoring work completion. Within a few weeks, Sarah was completing more assignments, attending classes without tardiness, and overall, she was much more pleasant at home, for the homework battles were minimized through Study Hall support. Sarah was able to complete most of her work at school when the Resource Room teacher reviewed her daily planner and directly assisted Sarah with additional processing time. Also, her teacher was tracking the assignments within the General Education classes daily. Sarah's success was directly aligned with her strengths (auditory learning) and supported by conscientious staff members who had strong organizational skills themselves.

Behavior: Some of the most bewildering students are those who qualify for the emotional behavior (EBD) disorder category. At the same time, often these students have some of the most extraordinary, elaborate gifts and talents. If I had to describe this group within one theme, it would be the proverbial square pegs/round holes phenomenon. When dealing with behavior, I tend to work from the position that behavior is a form of communication. The following story describes this situation well:

I had the opportunity to work with Lars's family in a suburban neighborhood in Western Washington. Lars, a middle school student, was adopted by his grandparents. According to his teachers, he was "emotionally disturbed," "a juvenile delinquent," "mentally ill," and "autistic." In fact, by the time I was hired by his grandparents to assist, Lars had already been suspended numerous times for angry outbursts. He told his grandparents that his teachers lied and frequently set him up to fail. In this situation, he perceived all the cards were stacked against him, for he felt the staff was looking to get him. He was either going to "shape up or be shipped out," according to staff I met with. Lars was not only a student with an emotional behavior disorder, he was an emotional wreck!

Fortunately, by the end of the year, he was enrolled in a new school that was founded upon the belief that their students can learn and they need structure, guidance, and most importantly, a chance to succeed. Many of this school's students entered with a special education plan identifying an emotional behavior component as a critical part. Back in June, when I spoke with the principal, I was assured that Lars would do well, for the program was geared toward students like him. In fact, the principal made it clear that the staff enjoyed working with complex students, who often saw success fairly quickly. The point of the program was to return the students to their home school as soon as possible.

A year passed, and I was invited to attend Lars's IEP meeting. Honestly, I was not looking forward to it; I was informed by his grandparents that the reason for the meeting was due to the school's closure. The school was sending their grandson back to his home school. I thought this was one of those budget crunch decisions, and Lars was being exited for the wrong reasons. Well, was I ever surprised!

Arriving a few minutes early, I had the opportunity to watch the staff in action. It was clear the teachers connected with their students through relationships first, then built curriculum upon student interests. The level of intimacy and mutual respect was evident in the brief conversations I overheard. This was encouraging. Then all of a sudden, Lars and his family entered the room. I was so taken back by his physical changes since I last saw him that I actually thought it was someone else sitting next to Lars's grandparents. This young man projected confidence and spoke in ways that were unlike the Lars I had previously met; there was nothing angry about him. In fact, he was both calm and actually in a playful mood with his parents and teachers. I listened with great intent to understand how this transformation took place.

When asked about the extraordinary changes as observed, Lars stated that the teachers were fair, he got along with everyone including staff, and they helped him feel he could do most anything he tried. In fact, the meeting was called by the teachers themselves, for they felt that Lars was ready to move on. Throughout the conversation, I was moved by the simple recipe established at this school:

- *Believe in their students' potential*

- *Create opportunities for academic and emotional (expressive) growth*

- *Build upon strengths, and*

- *Provide rigor and challenge in all instructional endeavors with structure and guidance*

When asked if he wanted to return to his old school, close to home, Lars responded with clarity, "That's the way it's supposed to work. I am supposed to be in General Education so I can move on."

Truthfully, I never imagined that Lars would have changed so quickly. But ever since the beginning, his grandparents always stated, "Lars is a good boy; he just needs someone to believe in him and give him a chance." During the previous school year, that opportunity was available. The staff and teachers at his new school believed in him and looked for the best in Lars at all times.

Lars's story expresses the most essential elements required within the complexity of EBD. It's all about relationships first and foremost, then establishing a safe environment with defined limits and structures, creating curriculum that incorporates student interests, and building upon strengths at all times. A fairly simple formula, but then again, this is not the case in many EBD-related IEP plans. From my experience, most often I see the following issues:

Limited understanding of the power of relationships as the primary fundamental connection between students and their learning environment. This is something that cannot be mandated, but the fundamental core is found within "true love," where understanding serves as the hub of all connections. Specifically, in working with complex cases, especially those that involve adoption, foster care, and attachment-related symptoms, the IEP and 504 process serve the student best by acknowledging life's most compelling needs: the desire to connect with others and a fundamental need to belong.

Poorly designed functional behavior analysis making a weak connection between antecedents and behavior; in fact, most FBA plans generically state "attention seeking" as the fundamental basis for the student's actions. Though most people bring good intentions to the traditional school setting, very few of them have the skillset of an experienced behavior analyst to pull off a well-written FBA. Too many times the FBA and related BIP are limited in scope and fail to truly make a difference.

I often recommend an independent education evaluation or an outside service provider with expertise in behavior analysis as a part of the IEP tool kit. We must always keep in mind the human experience is based upon two principles: "Everyone learns" and "Our actions are based upon what is in our perceived best interest." So an effective FBA and related BIP need to identify the link between these two principles for every student; there is never good reason for an effective FBA or BIP to fail if they are well written and followed through with intent.

Remedial curriculum; lacking student interest within the context of instruction. Here again, if a student is expected to spend hours and hours on what is perceived as "meaningless" or "boring" work, eventually the disconnect will present itself as students create their own curriculum (often highly disruptive). When challenged with engaging instruction, the creative mind feels a sense of engagement and fulfillment, and the student is willing to take on the less-desirable tasks often associated with traditional curriculum.

One of the extraordinary components of the EBD disability is how quickly the IEP process spirals out of control when a set of inconvenient behaviors takes center stage. The system seems to move at lightning speed when addressing containment and management of the student with EBD. But when it comes to addressing the needs of a typical student with learning disabilities, real change may take years to happen. Here's another story which makes this point, no matter how ridiculous it may appear.

Living and working on an island in Western WA has its positive sides. There appears to be a genuine sense of community in a town with a moat around it. On the other hand, when you don't seem to fit in with the community, there is nothing as lonely as feeling unwanted. Ricki was a middle school student with an ADHD diagnosis, and she brought with her all the usual suspects associated with this disability: impulsivity, distractibility, and a creative side. She loved to draw. She did not get along with the Resource Room teacher, for she felt like she could never do anything right in the eyes of her teacher. When it was fifth period each day and time for Resource Room, both Ricki and her teacher anxiously looked forward to their daily ritual of conflict and confrontation.

During the annual state assessment program, Ricki was sent to the library to participate in testing with the other kids with IEPs and 504s who needed an alternative setting. Within her peripheral range, Ricki immediately scanned the room for interesting books and quickly found her target—a how-to-draw book on display. Instead of doing the test with compliance and focus, like everyone else, Ricki decided to artistically fill in the bubbles on the multiple-choice test, complete the assessment early, and quickly move on to the book that caught her interest. She spent hours in the library learning how to draw cartoon characters rather than take the tests with serious intent. The Resource Room teacher was pleased as punch with Ricki during the assessment period, for Ricki was engrossed in the bubble designs on the test and then on the reading material. She was not a distraction to others, which was the teacher's main concern since Ricki was a very inconvenient child in the teacher's eyes. When interest calls, Ricki can spend hours and hours on things she loves. She loved drawing.

I was called in by the parent to assist with the IEP. A manifestation hearing was established when Ricki was expelled for those actions in the library during testing. Here's how it went: Ricki was so enthused about her latest drawings that she could not contain herself and had to show her teacher her recent artwork based upon the instructions provided by the book. Her teacher was mortified. The drawings, which later were revealed as quite similar to the illustrations in the how-to book, featured the Muppets, Cookie Monster, and other Jim Henson characters. One of the cartoons drawn by Ricki featured interaction between the Cookie Monster and an adult figure in confrontation with a Muppet character stating in a dialog bubble, "You are next." The artwork highlighted a gun in the Cookie Monster's hand, implying that the character was going to shoot the adult figure. As a result, things moved quickly: Ricki was emergency expelled on a "zero tolerance" policy, a manifestation hearing was immediately convened, and a prior written notice was implemented on her IEP. The team shifted her qualifying category from "health impairment" to "emotional behavior, disturbed" without the parent's support. Imagine how you would feel if this were your child going through the formal hearing involving such a silly matter as Cookie Monster and guns. My client was livid, and she frequently left the room in outbursts that included many expletives. Not only was I called in to manage the IEP end of the process, but I was also needed for anger management support. I will never forget one of my client's most compelling eruptions: "I was born and lived in Eastern Europe [former Soviet Union] my whole life where there were real guns every day. If you want to hear about real threats, I can tell you stories. Expelling my daughter for her cartoons, this is absolute bullsh*t. I can't take this anymore." She walked out several

126

times and slammed the door behind her, leaving the IEP team in a state of shock.

One of the things I tell parents on this path, especially within EBD advocacy, "Things often need to get worse before they get better." Sometimes it's best when the total support system crashes and the team has to pick up the pieces with a new mindset. In this case, it worked out great for Ricki. The team decided that she would be best served within a nonpublic agency private school featuring one-to-one instruction. This would all be paid for by the district. I was most impressed with the Resource Room teacher in this situation, for she basically hand-delivered a $40,000 a year educational program for Ricki. This event followed the well-publicized Columbine news story in Colorado. As a result, the teacher's union was fully aware of Ricki's actions and the possibility of more threats was too much for the district to bear. As expected, when we followed up months later with the private school, the director went on and on about how well Ricki was doing. Assignments were getting finished on time, and the teachers enjoyed her. "She is really creative and has lots of ideas to share ... we like her a lot!"

As stated earlier, within the realm of emotional behavior, it's all about relationship. The blessing found within these extraordinary cases is revealed within the challenge each provides. The true litmus test of love of teaching and love for students is discovered within the highly inconvenient situations each creates. Kids with EBD are not easy. Mother Theresa said it best: *"I know God will not give me anything I can't handle. I just wish that He didn't trust me so much."*

Simply, as in all IEP or 504 casework, our efforts are most effective through a lens highlighting potential and fundamentally grounded upon what already works. David Cooperrider, the father of *Appreciative Inquiry*, states it as follows: "*The arduous task of intervention will give way to the speed of imagination and innovation; and instead of negation, criticism, and spiraling diagnosis, there will be discovery, dream and design. ... And the metaphor speaking best to our primary task and role -- the child as the agent of inquiry -- is one where wonder, learning, and the dialogical imagination will be modus operandi.*"

Furthermore, Cooperrider makes the following statement as well, "*The [traditional paradigm] problem-solving approach directs attention to the 'worst of what is,' constantly examining what is wrong. The assumption is that if the problems are fixed, then the desired future will automatically unfold. In problem solving, it is assumed that something is broken, fragmented, not whole, and that it needs to be fixed. Thus the function of problem solving is to integrate, stabilize, and help raise to its full potential the workings of the status quo. By definition, a problem implies that one already has knowledge of what 'should be;' thus one's research is guided by an instrumental purpose tied to what is already known.*"

As stated in the beginning, the intent of this book is to encourage a new perspective within the IEP and 504 planning process. My paradigm is founded upon the five principles addressed within this book:

- **The initial steps begin by understanding the parent perspective, first and foremost.**

- **Second, shifting from ego and self-interest to understanding others is "true love" personified.**

- **During the initial stages of the collaborative process, "mutual understanding" remains your primary goal as you guide the team through the fundamental Evaluation and Present Levels of Performance.**

- **Through an evidence-based approach to decision making, you and your team make steady progress as you wade through collected data together, objectively.**

- **Finally, the benefits of your collective effort culminate within appreciative advocacy and a strength-based IEP and 504 Plan approach to intervention.**

Within the context of either the IEP or 504 intervention process, the synergistic magic available through collaboration and co-creativity supports an extraordinary transformation in the traditional group process. By working together, as one collaborative entity, something different unfolds within this paradigm shift. And this change is demonstrated through transparency, the glue that holds it all together!

Notes:

TRANSPARENCY: THE GLUE THAT HOLDS IT ALL TOGETHER

No matter how nice, kind, or welcoming you are, as long as there *appears* to be a veil between parents and school, you will always have a communication issue at the core of all special-needs discussions, including IEP and 504 Plan meetings. In contrast, when both sides of the intervention process bring to the table an open approach with full disclosure and willingness to explore all reasonable possibilities, the result is refreshing, transformative, and truly something rare to behold.

By letting go of the impulse to exclusively manage the decision process, transparency supports the intervention team since everyone is working from the same page (mutual understanding). Transparent communication requires a unique level of openness compared to traditional decision-making models. By surrendering control to the collective wisdom found within mutual understanding, the IEP/504 process takes a new direction. We can provide lip service to the principle of transparency, but walking the talk requires an authentic level of honesty that is not standard practice in most school districts. The practices of minimizing prognostic evaluations, establishing preconceived agendas before the collaborative process begins, and holding back information and services need to end for true transparency to take place and a new type of engagement to take hold.

Think of it this way: Do you really believe it is in YOUR best interest to take on the full responsibility of educating each child and going it alone, given these factors?

- *Shrinking budgets barely meeting basic education policies and guidelines*

- *Marginalization of rules, standards, and social morals once the founding pillars of culture and society*

- *Compliance replaced by hyper-interest and impulsivity*

- *Disabilities such as ADD, anxiety, and autism at alarming epidemic levels*

If you said, "YES," I am deeply sorry, for the path you are on looks more like a potential train wreck waiting to happen.

However, if you responded with "NO," we are on the same page.

I suggest we go back to the beginning and explore the fears that often guide the traditional special education process. By looking at ourselves, the uncertainties, and the worries that create walls, we can tear down the barriers between us. The following beliefs are often at the core of traditional site-based intervention as guided by staff:

- *"There are way too many kids being served within IEP or 504 Plans than what our system can handle; our caseloads are already at the maximum levels."*

- *"State and federal laws have established unreasonable mandates without appropriate funding; our hands are tied."*

There is truth in these statements. The system is set up to financially accommodate a percentage of students identified for IEP funding, but there is no direct funding available outside of a district for *all* potentially identified students, including 504 intervention. Currently, the number of students receiving specially designed instruction typically ranges between 10 and 15 percent of the student population. At the same time, we will continue to identify more students than the formula supports. Nevertheless, resources at the federal and state levels are available toward the "excess costs" associated with IEP expenses beyond the annual average per pupil expenditure (APPE). In Washington State, like most states, a *Safety Net* program is established, authorizing additional funding for excess costs, addressing IEP-supported student needs. For example, in the 2013-2014 school year, Washington State's Safety Net program offered school districts $32,000,000 in grant funding, with an average of $16,800 per award. Also, out of the 1,921 applications submitted, 86 percent of high-needs funding requests were awarded. This is not a deep-pockets resource with unlimited funding and without restrictions; however, it does make a difference!

Also, since General Education classrooms serve as the primary setting for most identified students, professional development and training all staff on the special-needs intervention process would likely be more cost-effective over the long haul than utilizing Special Education resources alone. Response to Intervention (RTI), a multitier approach to the early identification and support of students with learning and behavior needs, continues to be an effective tool utilized across the country. The RTI process begins with high-quality instruction and universal screening of all children in the General Education classroom. In my experience, schools which embrace RTI through General Education funding, support teachers through extensive professional development, and most notably, take on special-needs intervention from a "whole school" philosophy often manage the influx of identified special needs students more successfully than schools that use traditional programs.

Other barriers and attitudes that seem to get in the way of innovation and creativity include:

- *"We cannot manage the Special Education department within our budget limitations, compliance guidelines, and union contracts unless we implement intervention formulas and services within these parameters."*

- *"We cannot make everyone happy, nor will we meet the needs of all students. As a result, Due Process may be our only option."*

Again, there is truth to these statements as well. The Special Education system is pushed and pulled in many different directions, and financially the level of compliance guidelines and restrictions are extraordinary. Nevertheless, some of the most costly expenses within the IEP/504 process may be litigation and Due Process proceedings themselves in light of the financial burden expressed. Also, the negative impact of litigation on the working conditions within a school district takes its toll as well. Within the President's Commission on Excellence in Special Education Report (2002), the following findings were stated:

"Numerous parents, teachers and school administrators complained during the Commission's public sessions about the excessive focus on due process hearings and litigation over special education disputes. Disputes of all sorts divert parent and school time and money, and waste valuable resources and energy that could otherwise be used to educate children with disabilities. ... These threats create an adversarial atmosphere that severely limits the ability of parents and schools to cooperate. ... The threat of litigation alone has costs for teachers, students, and taxpayers. ... These costs and the dissatisfaction with the system merit serious reform" (U.S. Department of Education Office of Special Education and Rehabilitative Services).

As an education advocate, I meet Special Education directors all the time. I can tell you there are very few directors who lose their jobs for the reasons they are worried about: financial restraints and responsibilities. In fact, most of the directors and staff members who do get fired do so because they demonstrate significant flaws with poor communication and uncooperative relationships with staff, parents, or the community. As a result, conflicts of this magnitude can lead to litigation, whereas a number of these cases could have been avoided through cost-free transparency. On a recent survey conducted by Project Forum NASDSE, Special Education directors themselves were surveyed about attrition and frustrations associated with the position, and many mentioned the following concerns:

- *Spending a higher proportion of time and money on compliance/litigation matters*

- *Not receiving adequate administrative support and/or school board support*

- *Facing increasing budget constraints to meet district needs, and/or*

- *Confronting increased shortages of qualified personnel.*

From my point of view, there are a number of issues here that are within an administrator's scope of influence: "higher proportion of time on litigation [due process]," and "confronting increased shortages of qualified personnel." Both are directly tied to communication. I believe this reinforces the same points made I earlier: communication and relationship building are critical to the success of any Special Education director as well as every Special Education program.

By taking the high road and being genuine in our pursuit of partnership, the need for litigation significantly diminishes. Most skilled special education directors would agree that effective communication keeps a district out of Due Process in most cases. Also, qualified teachers choose to stay in a school district when they feel supported by administration and experience true partnership and collaboration with colleagues. In fact, Special Education teachers have higher turnover rates than any other group within education. I see this discrepancy as the result of an overemphasis on budget limitations, the burden of excessive paperwork, and work conditions requiring teachers "do more with less." Something needs to change. And I strongly believe we need to go back to square one: transparency—working in tandem with others through full disclosure—is the glue that holds all the parts in place. We are all in this mess together. True partnership between parents, staff, and community is best achieved through a transparent exchange of ideas and resources as well as relationship building. Once we let go of a false sense of control and surrender to something different, like collaboration and co-creativity, then we feel supported by something much stronger, much bigger than our individual selves—like the guiding principles of appreciative advocacy:

- *Understanding that there is an energy, a presence, or a source unifying each one of us.*

- *Faith in one another and the understanding that we can achieve much more as a group than as an individual.*

137

- *Belief that we are all an integral part of a larger mosaic-like puzzle; where we all influence one another, and present a unique gift within this experience called "life."*

- *Knowing our attitudes and beliefs shape our perceptions; "we see what we believe."*

Years ago, in my younger days as a new principal, my first day on the job ended up establishing itself as the "beginning of the end." I was never the same after meeting one of my parents; he is lovingly known throughout his community as "Slot Car Bob." Bob was not like anyone I had ever met before. His influence has been with me ever since; Bob taught me an extraordinary lesson about true partnership, transparency, and being authentic with others. Specifically, he forced the question upon me that each one of us in a leadership position must answer at some time: "Are we working together or are we working against one another?" You cannot have it both ways at your convenience in collaboration. It's one way or another, for true partnership requires a level of honesty, transparency, and trust atypical of the traditional "old school" paradigm.

During the interviews for the new principal position, numerous questions were asked, but the ones that seemed to stand out were those addressing parent and staff relations. Consistently, the questions' scenarios featured a so-called parent named "Bob." Eventually, I passed the test and was hired. One of the first tasks I was challenged with, according to the interview process, was to slay the dragon called "Bob," for he was a thorn in everyone's side at school. At least that's how the teachers and staff saw it.

On my first day as the new administrator, the school secretary came out from under her desk with a Cheshire cat grin. "Bob called and wants to set up an appointment to meet with you today." I spoke with him immediately on the phone, and we set up an appointment for later that morning. One of the first things that caught my attention was his voice; he came across sounding like Popeye, gruff and with conviction. I had the distinct impression he was a large man with a loud voice who carried himself with a swagger.

When I first met Bob, I was taken aback by the reality of the guy. He was nothing like I imagined—except the voice. He was on the short side, had a medium build, and looked like someone I would drink a beer with. He obviously cared deeply about his two kids, who attended my school. He also loved slot car racing. "I have a first grader and a third grader," he told me after shaking hands with a firm grip. He immediately put his cards on the table: "I am one of those house husbands you read about. My wife works the airlines, and my primary responsibility at home is to make sure the kids get the best first and third grade experience at school. So I am here for them."

After a number of questions and answers going back and forth across the table, as we sized one another up, he pulled no punches and stated, "I know your teachers and what they can and cannot do. They all have their strengths and weaknesses. That's where you come in. I need you to work with them to assure my kids get the best education possible, for they only have this one shot at first and third grade. It's fairly simple: Are you going to work with me or against me? It's a matter of choice. Whose team are you on?"

As I said, this was the "beginning of the end." Bob laid it out as clearly as possible: Who do I work for? Either I work for the teachers and keep parents like him at bay, or I work for the community in support of learning. I looked across the table and told him *something like, "I am here to assure the best learning experience for all students." He looked at me again. "Don't give me this bullsh*t. I know what you are up against. So I want to know now, are you working with me or against me in support of my kids?" There was no going back. He wanted to know with conviction where I stood in light of leadership, supervision, and commitment. I looked at him directly, put out my hand, and stated, "I am working with you." I've never looked back ever since. He knew it and so did I. If you are going to talk about partnership and transparency, you either walk the talk or get out altogether. Anything less is not honest.*

Fortunately, Bob and I got along very well; like I said, he reminded me of someone I knew. Possibly, I saw a bit of myself in Bob. He was one of the most dedicated parents I have ever worked with in thirty-plus years of education. He never backed down from the fight. He also knew his responsibilities as a parent and took them to heart.

One of the best things I learned about Bob was he never gave up; he was tenacious. For example, a couple years later, he realized the district next door ran a better program for students; their test scores were light years ahead of ours. So he approached the district with a proposal: The only way his kids could attend the school was if he moved into the district's boundary or if he was an employee. And he wasn't going to move across the street to the neighboring district. He proposed an employment contract that today would never fly, but Bob was one who never gave up. His proposal included a set number of hours as an instructional aide working within the school in whatever capacity needed. For this, he was to be paid a dollar, and his kids would be able to attend the school. This was approved by the superintendent,

140

for he too realized you were either on Bob's team or not. The choice was ours.

True to my first impression of Bob, I always saw him as a straight shooter. He did not hold back, and his actions were in direct alignment with supporting his kids and their learning. Sure he was working from personal interest, supporting his kids first and foremost, but he was willing to take everyone else with him on this adventure as well. Nothing was left off the table, and it was always a matter of straight talk and nothing less. I learned a lot from Bob. I have always appreciated the example he set years ago. We all need someone like Bob to set us straight when it comes to transparency. You cannot have it both ways; either you play your hand honestly, with full disclosure, or you are misleading others through appearances alone. You need to walk the talk!

* * *

Walking the Talk: Honesty in the Face of Transparency

You have made it so far and now, you are called upon to address three basic questions:

- *Do you see a need for a new paradigm and a fresh perspective to unfold within your school's IEP and 504 processes?*

- *Are you open to the possibility of taking a new direction within your school or district's program?*

- *If so, what are you already doing that resembles the following course of action?*

141

The initial steps begin by **understanding the parent perspective first and foremost**. Genuine collaboration and partnership begin with understanding another's perspective. Specifically, your success as a teacher depends on the relationships you create with parents and within the context of IEP and 504 Plan development. School-to-home partnership is your starting point.

Second, **shifting from ego and self-interest to understanding others** is "true love" personified. If you truly love your job and the kids, an authentic demonstration of this highlights acceptance and unconditional appreciation of others. Anything less is not love and compassion; rather, it's more about selfish interest and control. You may love your job or your students, but true love is demonstrated by understanding first and foremost. Simply, an open heart creates the context of partnership, and an open mind supports collaboration.

During the initial stages of the collaborative process, **mutual understanding remains your primary goal** as you guide the team through the fundamental Evaluation and Present Levels of Performance. By creating common ground through a collaborative set of understandings and insights about the student, the team navigates the intervention process in one cohesive direction. Without mutual understanding, your foundation will fail.

Through **an evidence-based approach to decision making**, you and your team make steady progress as you wade through collected data together, objectively. By separating emotion and subjectivity from the process, putting agendas and self-interest off the table, the team is better able to move forward with solid decisions, interventions, and innovative ideas based upon data and quantifiable evidence.

Furthermore, the benefits of your collective effort culminate within appreciative advocacy: **a strength-based IEP and 504 Plan approach to intervention**. By doing this, you are creating bridges toward success. People achieve so much more individually as well as collectively from a positive "what works" perspective. In addition, appreciative advocacy highlights that "Every child is a gift waiting to unfold," and inspires extraordinary innovation and creativity within the intervention process due to the overarching principles of promise and potential. As such, your efforts will translate to IEP and 504 Plans that work and support student learning.

Finally, **genuine collaboration and cooperation develop within the context of transparency**, revealing open disclosure of information and hidden agendas, including "hold back" conditions. By letting go of the impulse to manage the decision process toward expected outcomes, transparency supports an open approach to communication between stakeholders. As a result, resourcefulness, creativity, and innovation will prosper.

Notes:

EPILOGUE: OUT OF THE MOUTHS OF BABES

So I ask: "Are you a part of the solution, part of a collaborative-transparent process, or are you more "business as usual," and by choice supporting instead the fear-based scarcity paradigm? Again, are you working with me or against me? That's the same question Bob confronted me with many years ago.

Sure, "Are you working with me?" sounds simple. But I truly understand it's not always easy or black and white when both the institution and culture of education are founded upon "We've always done it this way" traditions as well as "Why reinvent the wheel?" belief systems. Obviously there are very large hurdles to overcome. However, the time has come for change, and a paradigm shift is inevitable. If this shift doesn't take place within, I can guarantee you that change will happen in spite of us! The children who need our help are <u>already</u> within our classrooms, and something needs to be done. Quickly!

In 2015, I was given the opportunity to return to the classroom as a middle school seventh grade teacher. I took on this challenge because I wanted to see for myself what teachers face every day within today's classrooms. And I am deeply grateful for what I learned during this experience.

During a five-period schedule, I was assigned to two classes identified as "Highly Capable" while my three other periods were General Education classes. In contrast to the gifted classes, the three GE classes had a wide range of student profiles, including developmentally delayed students who were supported with an instructional assistant through inclusion as well as a potpourri of "typical" middle school kids. What caught my attention from the first day was the number of students who were within the General Education program that did not have either a 504 Plan or an IEP but who demonstrated an alarming set of academic deficits and emotional needs.

For example, the optional nature of "homework" was something I was not prepared for. Most of the Highly Capable kids did their assignments every night. They had internalized the idea that grades matter, and homework was an important part of their intrinsic desire to do well in school. However, within the General Education classes, the notion of homework was clearly something that most of my students avoided with an endless stream of excuses. Now, I did not hear anything that resembled "My dog ate it" or "I did it but I accidentally threw it in the trash." But what many of students told me broke my heart, for they were clearly guided by a different set of circumstances than their Highly Capable peers were:

"Mr. Davis, my parents really don't care if I do my homework or not; I am supposed to babysit my brothers and that's good enough for them".

146

"I hate homework; why do we have to do school stuff all day and then at night?"

"I don't do my homework because I am in my room crying about my mom and dad."

"I try to remember my assignments but I can't. Really, by the time I get home, I just forget everything. Then, my parents yell at me for not having homework."

"Even though it may not seem like it, some of us have major problems and we have a lot going on in our lives. It could be that one kid who is always smiling and laughing and talking in class, Yeah, you may not know it but a lot of us including myself struggle with some pretty big problems ... so when you punish us for not getting our work done, maybe it's because we literally can't."

*This was just the tip of the iceberg. I was also taken back by the number of my students who expressed emotional trauma and anxiety as though those significant things were nothing more than a common cold. Daily, students would come to me and openly share how they felt about school, themselves, and life in general. These comments as well as the ones below were on a writing assignment called **What would you like your teachers to know?***

"I would like my teachers to know that I feel like I am always making mistakes and I'm never good enough."

"I haven't seen my dad in a long time and I am dealing with loss and grief."

147

"It's hard for me to pay attention and focus 'cause I have different mental disorders, like anxiety, bipolar, and depression, so I am constantly talking and fidgeting 'cause I am trying to keep my mind off of it. I also fidget for I have ADHD. I don't like to talk about it ... so no one suspects it but every once in a while I'll just break down and cry. I don't know why."

"I live with my Uncle and Aunt because I used to be in an abusive situation. I'm never confident about anything I do. "

Fortunately, all my classes were designed upon a gifted education project-based approach, no matter where the kids fell academically. Both Highly Capable classes and General Education provided opportunities to build upon their interests and creativity. So they were all encouraged to learn through their strengths. However, I did notice within the first days of school that almost half of my General Education students had already established a belief that they were poor students and were not good at school. I observed in the following weeks an extraordinary number of students demonstrating executive functioning deficits, including poor working memory, impulse control issues, limited organization and planning skills, and hyper-focus toward interests-alone; which often never presented at school for there were few tasks and assignments which captured the student's interest at heart. Also, the number of students, with ADHD-like tendencies, particularly boys, was almost epidemic. So it was my challenge to incorporate the students' interests into the assignments and projects as best as possible. Differentiation goes way beyond skill levels when teaching requires "interest-based learning." Then again, for so many of my students, like with yours, if you don't have a meaning-centered hook, then it is almost impossible to capture their attention.

So here's the plan*

No matter how you look at change, especially institutional paradigm shifts, real change evolves when the following elements are clearly in place. (*see the Addendum: Planning Guide)

- Fundamentally, there must be a **reason for change**; usually some form of cognitive dissonance between "what is" and "what should be" presents itself. With IEP and 504 procedures and practices currently in place in most schools, however you look at it, the current business as usual model of intervention fails to meet the needs of too many students. The evidence clearly shows that IEP and 504 plan-supported students continue to struggle year after year. You know it, and I know it. Something needs to change. On a personal level, Special Education teachers leave the profession at alarming rate compared to their General Education colleagues; the research addresses this issue in volumes. Also, the extensive number of Special Education job openings compared with General Education vacancies indicate a pattern as well. I see it simply: within the old paradigm, Special Education staff are expected to do the impossible daily. They must work miracles with limited resources and with minimal support from administration and General Education staff. Most notably, Special Education personnel are expected to support a flawed system. As a result, burnout will continue and turnover will plague every school district. So, why not try something new as described in this book? Begin fresh with a rejuvenated perspective, one student at a time. We all want to feel like our efforts make a difference. That alone is reason for change!

- Furthermore, for change to last the test of time, **a well-established vision needs to take shape**. And that's where this book serves its purpose: to help you and your school or district explore a new school of thought within IEP and 504 intervention process. However, this book is not a "how-to" step-by-step recipe workbook. A more in-depth vision of your classroom, your school, or your district will be required for real change to evolve. Whether we call it a "mission statement," a site-based "school improvement plan," or "district initiative," all stakeholders must embrace this vision. The intent of this book is to support a vision of what intervention can look like from a collaborative framework. The specific "how-to" nuts and bolts required to get there is either within the resources found in your school, your district, or within another book all together.

- Also, research addressing systemic change, both at the individual and institutional level, highlights **goal setting within an effective change process**. Not only does the vision need to be clear, but the steps toward implementation need to be specific and precise, highlighting well- defined goals, objectives, due dates, personal responsibilities, and accountability. This is very doable and within your wheelhouse.

- Finally, real changes, such as those proposed within this book, require **a well-established support system**. Today, most districts are exploring the development of "Professional Learning Communities" at the site level, which support student learning but ultimately also help staff support one another through institutional change. The fundamental shift here is found within the professional relationships amongst staff. It's imperative that you find a like-minded colleague who's willing to take on change in a big way. Often, change like this creates stress. Working with colleagues through a heart-centered, meaningful sense of community can provide support during this transformative shift. Richard DuFour, one of the leading practitioners of Professional Learning Communities, makes the following statement:

"The professional learning community model flows from the assumption that the core mission of formal education is not simply to ensure that students are taught but to ensure that they learn. This simple shift—from a focus on teaching to a focus on learning—has profound implications for schools. School mission statements that promise "learning for all" have become a cliché. But when a school staff takes that statement literally—when teachers view it as a pledge to ensure the success of each student rather than as politically correct hyperbole—profound changes begin to take place".

Surely, a revolutionary paradigm shift will require time and patience. The development of a collaborative intervention process is similar to a creative process like art or music; intervention and innovation are a form of artistic expression found within the relationships we consciously develop. Michelangelo didn't create *David* in one day, nor did the Gustave Eiffel create his tower overnight. Creating a relationship-inspired intervention process with our colleagues, students, and their parents will also take time.

Most notably, change of this magnitude is a matter of choice. Our lives are an ongoing process, and the choices we make each day can recreate and rejuvenate our lives. On the other hand, if we hold on to "doing business as usual" and remain reluctant to change, these belief systems may cause us to dig in deeper within our set ways, and we feel even more stuck. Our actions and our choices are guided by the following perspectives.

- **Ego**: Working from a self-centered perspective, fear, or worry often take center stage within the core of the egocentric belief system. Unfortunately, the old paradigm of IEP and 504 development often reflects this perspective due to resource scarcity, economic restraints, and job security concerns. I have attended way too many intervention meetings where the agenda is driven by selfish interest cloaked by "doing what's best for the kids."

- **Experience**: Good old experience and wisdom often guide our understanding of each child within the intervention process. And in fact, tried-and-true strategies and best practices often hit the target. Nevertheless, this paradigm is limited, for it is grounded in the past. Today, many kids require something altogether different, so what once worked years ago may miss the mark. Today's kids bring to the classroom a whole new range of issues, concerns, complexities, and most importantly, gifts and talents. As a result, the intervention process requires a fresh perspective. Every child's path is unique and necessitates innovation founded upon a true collaborative process that taps into the vast resources found within many rather than only a few. Years ago, schools were expected to do it alone. Today, we have to work in partnership and build upon our collective wisdom and experience to make the best decisions.

- **Inspiration**: This is where this book truly takes shape and shines within the intervention process: As we are guided by the idea that every child is a gift, we open ourselves to the possibility of potential. And by doing so, the IEP/504 team can reach way beyond the traditional scope of resources, innovations, and creativity. True partnership and synergy develop when everyone at the table is inspired by a common premise of faith and inspiration. We find ourselves uplifted by the promise found within each child. Also, knowing that the intervention team *itself* is a gift makes a huge difference. This understanding projects an indelible mark on the school learning environment. As Anne Frank eloquently stated, "Everyone has inside himself a piece of good news! The good news is that you really don't know how great you can be, what you can accomplish, and what your potential is."

153

As a staff member of the middle school instructional team, I felt like I was an important part of something larger than myself. In fact, what made our program unique was the underlying belief that we were collaborating. Self-interest was not a part of the teaching experience at our school, for our administrative leaders made it clear from day one: "It's all about team." Also, most interesting was the composition of the staff: most of us were older, veteran teachers and educators with a wealth of teaching and life experience. Though there were a lot of big personalities among our staff, there weren't any big egos on board. In fact, it was fascinating to be a part of a team that functioned "as one." I remember our principal calling out many times, "We're all in this together, team."

Honestly, at times teaching was a challenge for me. It wasn't the endless hours of lesson planning or the kids that caused me strife. It was the feeling of being caught between a rock and a hard place that wore me down over time. On one hand, I truly believed I needed to spend more time on curriculum; I felt I was always running behind. On the other hand, I deeply felt the need to spend more time developing relationships with the students. Their issues, their concerns, and their dreams went way beyond the content of my lessons. And I felt torn by the proverbial conflict: head or heart.

*I could not solve this alone. So one day after school, I spoke to my principal about this feeling of being caught in the middle. Diane was not only an experienced administrator, she was also someone who loved teaching. I trusted her judgment. After about five minutes describing my situation, she just looked at me and smiled. And I will never forget what she said: "What do **you** remember from seventh grade?"*

And simply, it all came together as I left her office: It's about relationships, creating meaningful experiences along the way, and discovering the gift within. Nothing more and nothing less.

We are all in this together. However, we have a choice: Do we move forward as one or alone? Either you are an essential part of the solution as described through this book, or you are supporting the problem caused by business-as-usual practices. It's like that famous line: "You can't be a little bit pregnant." Same thing goes for authentic partnership, collaboration, and transparency—it's either one way or the other. You can't be a little bit transparent. As Slot Car Bob stated it so poignantly, "Are you on the team?" I hope so. For the transformative ideas presented within *Love, Understanding, and Other Best Practices* are more about attitude changes and perception shifts than any other form of change. **What you believe is what you see.**

However you decide, I know one thing for sure: The number of children who will be touched by your guidance, your support, and your love, will be astounding.

Blessings to you.

Larry Martin Davis

ADDENDUM

Key Words and Phrases:
Special Education System Fundamentals:

Free Appropriate Public Education (FAPE): The Section 504 regulation requires a school district to provide a "free appropriate public education" to each qualified person with a disability who is in the school district's jurisdiction, regardless of the nature or severity of the person's disability.

Individuals with Disabilities Act (IDEA): A law ensuring services are provided to children with disabilities throughout the nation. IDEA governs how states and public agencies provide early intervention, Special Education and related services to more than 6.5 million eligible infants, toddlers, children, and youth with disabilities.

Title I support: Educational supports provided by the federal government for disadvantaged students requiring intervention in critical learning areas; an extension of General Education.

Response to Intervention (RTI): A multi-tier approach to the early identification and support of students with learning and behavior needs. The RTI process begins with general education instruction and universal screening of all children.

Section 504 Plan: Educational support provided for identified students with disabilities through accommodations within the General Education program; requires an annual review.

Specially Designed Instruction and Individualized Education Plan (IEP): Specially designed instruction for identified students provided by district special education services following a formal evaluation process.

Evaluation:

Evaluation: Formal process usually conducted by a school psychologist to explore potential disabilities and their impact on learning; outside evaluations may be utilized within this process.

Discrepancy model: Within the Evaluation, a comparison between ability based upon IQ scores and achievement as measured by various assessment tests, typically using standard scores between 90 and 110 as the "average" range; to qualify for Specific Learning Disabilities:

Specific learning disability: (may include, but not limited by the following)

Reading Comprehension: The ability to read text and process and understand its meaning.

Reading Fluency: The speed with which someone reads text.

Reading Symbol Recognition: The ability to interpret reading letters and symbols.

Math Computation: The ability to apply basic functions: add, subtract, divide, multiply.

Math Problem Solving: The ability to utilize computation within real applications.

Written Expression: The ability to write down information and ideas (using sentences, paragraphs, correct grammar, and spelling) such that the intent of the author is clear and can be understood by others. It is a complex process that involves organization, structuring sentences, correct grammar, and correct spelling.

Health Impairment, Other: According to IDEA, Other Health Impairment is defined as having limited strength, vitality, or alertness, including a heightened alertness to environmental stimuli, that results in limited alertness with respect to the educational environment, that is due to chronic or acute health problems such as asthma, attention deficit disorder or attention deficit hyperactivity disorder, diabetes, epilepsy, a heart condition, hemophilia, lead poisoning, leukemia, nephritis, rheumatic fever, and sickle cell anemia; and adversely affects a child's educational performance. An alternative means to qualify for SDI.

Other Qualifying Conditions:

Autism.

Blindness.

Deafness.

Emotional Disturbance.

Hearing Impairment.

Intellectual Disability.

Multiple Disabilities.

Orthopedic Impairment.

Traumatic Brain Injury.

Essential Elements of an IEP:

Present Levels of Performance: Current state of a student's progress highlighted by evidence, assessments, and observations.

Goals: Specific learning targets based upon the identified areas requiring specially designed instruction: "moving from [point a] ... to [point b] ... as measured by ..."

Service matrix: Identifies the services, related support, and the minutes provided in support of the specially designed instruction.

Extended School Year (ESY): Additional services over the summer in situations where extraordinary regression or loss of skills would take place during the break.

Behavior: The Inconvenient Truth with Special Education:

Executive functioning (EF): Executive functioning (and self-regulation) are the mental processes that enable us to plan, focus attention, remember instructions, and juggle multiple tasks successfully. ADD/ADHD as well as autism diagnoses present organization and planning challenges associated with EF.

Functional Behavior Assessment (FBA): A behavioral assessment is generally a problem-solving process for addressing student behavior. The process relies on a variety of techniques and strategies to identify the purposes of specific behavior and to help teams select interventions to directly address the problem behavior. In theory, the team is trying to understand the purpose of the behavior and follow up with interventions to increase positive behavior and diminish disruption.

Behavior Intervention Plan: The specific plan of action following a FBA; includes the following:

Describes the problem behavior

161

The reasons the behavior occurs

The intervention strategies that will address the problem behavior.

Manifestation hearing: When a child with an identified disability, supported through a 504 or an IEP, engages in behavior or breaks a school code of conduct and the school proposes to remove the child, the school must hold a hearing to determine if the child's behavior was caused by his disability. This hearing, known as a manifestation hearing, is a process to review the relationship between the child's disability and the behavior, guided by the evidence presented.

Collaborative Decision Making:

Consensus: Group decision-making process in which group members develop and agree to support a decision in the best interest of the whole.

Mutual understanding: A relation of affinity or harmony between people; whatever affects one correspondingly affects the other; all for one and one for all.

Evidence-based decision: Evolved from medical culture; emphasizes a rational, objective, and empirical/data approach to addressing issues and decisions.

Procedural safeguards:

Dispute resolution resources available to parents guided by state and federal laws including:

162

Mediation: A process facilitated by a neutral, non-biased third party when both parents and school districts agree to work toward a collaborative resolution.

Independent Education Evaluation: An outside evaluation, paid for by the district, provided to the parents when the district-developed evaluation is in question.

Citizen's complaint: A formal complaint based upon IDEA/FAPE guidelines presented by parents or other informed parties typically presented to the state or regional offices.

Due Process: Either the parent/adult student or the school district has the right to request a Due Process hearing whenever there is a dispute between the parent and the school district over the district's proposal or refusal to initiate or change the identification, evaluation, proposed IEP or portion thereof, the implementation of the IEP, educational placement, or the provision of a free appropriate public education (FAPE). Simply, it's when a resolution case goes before a judge.

Notes:

THE NEW SCHOOL OF THOUGHT IEP & 504 PLANNING GUIDE:

School or Organization:

Reasons for Change: *Why are we considering doing this? What would be gained by doing so?*

_____

_____

_____

Resources for Change: *What already works? What success are we building upon?*

_____

_____

_____

How do we currently support one another in times of change and transformation? *What already works?*

_____

_____

_____

Imagine: What could it look like? The vision ...

- Communication:

_____

_____

_____

- Mutual Understanding:

_____

_____

_____

- Evidence-Based Decision Making:

_____

_____

_____

- Strength-Based Interventions:

_____

_____

_____

- Transparency:

_____

_____

_____

Incremental Steps Toward Change: *What will each sub-step look like?*

Goals: Measured by: Due by*:   Responsibilities by: Resources:

_____   _____   _____   _____   _____

_____   _____   _____   _____   _____

_____   _____   _____   _____   _____

_____   _____   _____   _____   _____

_____   _____   _____   _____   _____

_____   _____   _____   _____   _____

Success and Celebrations* (check in points): *Woo-Hoo!*

Dates: _____

Dates: _____

Dates: _____

Dates: _____

Areas of Improvement*: *What next?*

_____

_____

_____

BELATED THANK YOU

Throughout this book, I have referred to a number of valuable references I treasure. Likely, you have your own favorites. As I shared before, *Love, Understanding, and Other Best Practices* is more about encouraging you to pursue your vision—and to tap into your team's talents, insights, and ingenuity—than about providing you with set of tried-and-true resources.

However, there are a number of resources I believe are noteworthy, for they have significantly influenced the development of this book. I am grateful and much appreciative of their impact on my career, my life, and my ability to serve in this capacity.

Special-needs parents: Without you, your trust, and the lessons you have taught me on this path, I would have had nothing to share. For my growth as a person, as well as an educator, is directly tied to the experiences we have in common. Most importantly, the love you express toward your children, no matter what challenges you have faced, has deeply influenced my life. For it is within your desire to do what's best for your child, as well as your ability to let go and trust the process much greater than you, where I have learned the most. This book is founded upon faith. Thank you.

HeartMath: I used to be a person who took pride in knowing I *knew* things. I was more head than heart. However, through the years, I have discovered the importance of a balanced approach toward life, which includes relationships at the core of my personal and professional life. Also, I fully understand the need for life's greatest decisions to also come from a balanced perspective of head and heart. And this is where HeartMath comes in.

In 2010, I participated in an introduction training session, and literally, within seconds, I knew that HeartMath would be an important part of my advocacy toolkit. The primary purpose of HeartMath lies in the underlying mission supporting wellness, emotional coherence, and social harmony on a global level. Immediately afterwards, I pursued training so I could share the emotional resilience and wellness resources with my clients. Most notably, throughout the years these heart-centered strategies have become an important part of my life and are integrated into each day. I highly recommend Heartmath.org for you and your colleagues. The essential tools for developing a relationship-inspired district and school are available free or at very little cost: HeartMath research-based practices and wellness strategies are universal and timeless, like breath!

Carmel Topinka: Likely, you don't know Carmel. But if you did, you would admire and love her like I do. She is one of those people who truly understands the notion of living a heart-inspired life. She also brings to my life an extraordinary talent for seeing details when I often just see the big picture. (Here again, the importance of balance stands out.) This book, as well as the complimentary handbook, *Insider's Guide to Special Education Advocacy* (written for parents), would never be in your hands if not for Carmel's editing talents and unyielding patience reading every "last draft" time after time. Thank you, dear!

"No problem can be solved from the

same level of consciousness that created it.

We must learn to see the world anew."

Albert Einstein*

* Seems like he knew what he was talking about!